#Startfirst

D0957465

Passionista

noun | pas·sion·is·ta | \'pa-shən-ēs-tä\

- A woman who pursues her passion(s) as a career with a thirst for continuous growth and a desire to serve others.

- A female entrepreneur who courageously seeks happiness above all else while making the world a better place.

- A woman with big ambition and a success mindset who pursues happiness and serves others by turning her passion(s) into a paycheck.

See Also: Boss Babe, Girl Boss, Lady Boss, Badass, Doer, Fashionista, Role Model, Mentor, Entrepreneur, Success

Published by
Lessons From Network
www.LessonsFromNetwork.com

Distributed by
Lessons From Network
P.O. Box 93927
Southlake, TX 76092
817-379-2300
www.LessonsFromNetwork.com/books

© Copyright by Lessons From Network 2016

All rights reserved worldwide. No part of this book may be reproduced or transmitted in any form or by any means, electronic or mechanical, including photocopying, recording, or by any information storage and retrieval system, without the written permission of the publisher, except where permitted by law.

ISBN: 978-0-9983125-0-7   (Paperback)

Printed in the United States of America.

PASSIONISTAS

Tips, Tales and Tweetables From Women Pursuing Their Dreams

Join The Passionistas Facebook community

Share with us your testimonials, comments and more.
For updates and Passionista news
LIKE our page at Facebook.com/Passionistasbook

Also

Receive Your Special Bonuses For
Buying the Passionistas Book!

Access multiple Free Gifts from Erika De La Cruz,
Kyle Wilson (the publisher) and more!

Go to www.PassionistaBook.com

Or send an email to
info@lessonsfrompassionistas.com
with Gifts in the subject

To order additional copies, including quantity discounts, of **Passionistas: Tips, Tales and Tweetables From Women Pursuing Their Dreams** see below.

SPECIAL QUANTITY PRICING:
(Retail $17.97)

1	$12.97 ea
2-9	$9.97 ea
10-24	$6.97 ea
25-99	$5.47 ea
100+	$3.97 ea

Plus shipping. Based on location and weight.

TO ORDER PLEASE:

1. *Order online www.LessonsFromNetwork.com/Books

2. Call 817-379-2300

2. E-Mail: info@lessonsfromnetwork.com

4. Via mail: **Lessons From Network**
   P.O. Box 93927
   Southlake, TX 76092

You can mix and match these additional titles:

- *The Little Black Book of Fitness: Tales from Mind, Body & Soul Warriors*
- *Mom & Dadpreneurs: Stories, Strategies and Tips of Super Achievers in Family and Business!*
- *The Daily Difference: Life Lessons to Achieve More*.

*Order online at www.LessonsFromNetwork.com/Books and receive over 10 additional bonuses from Erika De La Cruz, Kyle Wilson and more!

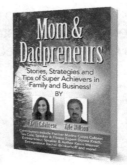

Order online www.LessonsFromNetwork.com/Books

FOREWORD

I've always been attracted to talented and passionate people who create things. Whether it is music, athletics, entertainment, business, etc., being a part of creating something pulls me in. That's what attracted me to the seminar world and the opportunity to fill up large rooms of people looking for inspiration and wisdom. Eventually fate would bring me to a partnership with Jim Rohn and an 18 year journey that continues to amaze me. It was my privilege to be responsible for getting his message out to the world; millions of people's lives were changed by his message. That relationship led to other partnerships with giants in the seminar and personal development world like Brian Tracy, Mark Victor Hansen, Darren Hardy Les Brown, Og Mandino and others.

You may notice the above list is all men. The truth is that the larger seminar world has been mostly a male driven world.

Which brings me to Passionistas!

How I met Erika De La Cruz was as serendipitous as how this project came together. Her lane was very much in the entertainment world. She was a lightening rod and was making things happen. Yet, what impressed me the most was her philosophy, attitude, and work ethic. She was out hustling, and yet knew her greatest success would come from giving and serving. This millennial seemed wise beyond her years.

She assured me there were more where she came from: millennial women out chasing their dreams, overcoming all kinds of challenges, yet committed to taking the necessary risk to follow the path they committed to.

From there, the Passionistas book was born, a vehicle to share so many of the amazing stories of women, both millennials and Gen Xers, who are at the top of their professions or may just be getting started on the journey but have already had some amazing lessons they are able to share, and more importantly impact thousands and hopefully millions of women that will read this book.

This started out as an idea and a hope. Now I can say 100% I'm a FAN! I'm a fan of Erika De La Cruz and I'm a fan of these 39 women and their stories and lessons.

This book is not just a compilation of feel good, life has always been great, here is my best day on Facebook stories. No, what you are about to read are some very gritty, from the heart, often born out of adversity, stories that I promise will inspire and make you better!

I've cried, I've laughed, and I have felt more determined than ever to follow my dreams and passion while reading these stories. And I'm NOT this book's demographic at all.

It will be my mission for women of all ages, in particular teens and millennials, to experience these 39 powerful women and their authentic, from-the-heart stories. This book will touch and relate to exactly what the reader may be going through with some powerful tips and inspiration on how to get through obstacles they encounter and come out the other side more determined and validated than ever.

All I ask is read the first story, then another, and another. See where your heart takes you. See if you see yourself in the women sharing their struggles, their victories, their lessons. You will be moved! You will be lifted up! You will be inspired!

Then make sure and take action. Don't just be an observer. Make sure, like these 39 women, you get in the game. Your game. You are the lead actor in your own movie.

And if these stories impact you, Erika, the contributors, and I ask for you to then share this book with other women. With mothers, sisters, daughters, granddaughters, friends, and with young entrepreneurs looking for a road map and ideas.

As the publisher of this book, I'm proud of the women and the stories we are sharing. Everyone involved has put a lot of work and energy into making sure this book and the lessons inside it will make a positive difference and a ripple in the world. We are honored that you are taking the time to read and helping start that ripple.

I salute Erika and every passionista in this book for being vulnerable, yet brave, and for wanting to make a difference through their unique message and lessons in the the world.

Enjoy!

Kyle Wilson, Founder LessonsFromNetwork.com, Jim Rohn Int, YourSuccessStore and KyleWilson.com. Co-Author Chicken Soup for the Entrepreneur's Soul

TABLE OF CONTENTS

Dedication

For Sho Sho. For Ashley & for Nicole.

Because of you, even from the darkest places,

I only expect that light comes next.

Acknowledgement

To Bethney Bonilla & Takara Sights:

The best editors in the "boss babe business."

From your brilliance, these pages have come to life.

INTRODUCTION

Passionistas—the stories, the book, the authors—the entire brand itself is a testament of a dream, coming to fruition. (And surprisingly, it was unintentional!)

It began four years ago, when I was still in a comfortable corporate world by day, but dreaming of somehow building a personal brand, comprised of all the things I loved to do and crafting some sort of career from it (entrepreneurship). Each month, I'd receive at my doorstep my source of inspiration, a copy of the latest issue of *Marie Claire*. I'd immediately flip through the pages, past the seasonal trends, and stop right before the beauty section at a monthly printed series called "**@Work**."

This small section of the magazine featured women killing it in their industries, but more importantly, the publication never failed to share the women's initial setbacks and included hacks and tips to pursue the reader's own passion. Those pages made my dream seem so tangible and so much closer than the other feeds I had access to—where bloggers seemed to wake up, be carried on a magic cloud to their careers, sip from perfect coffee cups, change outfits all day and then be re-touched by the magic "filter-wand." No! I wanted to know HOW they built their dreams, WHAT they had to go through before the business and WHY my goals were just as likely to happen if I set my mind to it. And then one issue arrived and through the text, I found a word, seemingly overlooked—"Passionista." I immediately cut out the clipping, pasted it to my dream board and, well, forgot about it.

However, within the year, I broke off into my actual dreams full-throttle: entertainment and personal brand pursuits, TV gigs, red carpet, and a series of business models for my hosting and coaching programs. Through that journey—I began sharing my real story, one of a few trials and tribulations. Most importantly, I vowed to remain authentic. Each time I was featured in the media, or even through conversation I'd use the term *Passionista*, "well, I think of myself as a Passionista, I'm pursuing my passion, maintaining my interests, while also inspiring others and generating revenue." Readers and publications LOVED it; I started being referred to as "The Passionista."

And thus, when I met a gentleman by the name of Kyle Wilson—a renowned industry giant and thought leader, founder of Your Success Store and partner to one of the most Inspirational Men in history, Jim Rohn, I was shocked and elated that our missions aligned! He aimed to share his story "The Man Behind the Legend—Jim Rohn," the truthful, personality-filled story, debunking the belief that success happens overnight. Through him sharing, I was re-inspired to teach and coach the boss babes I was working with at the time. I kept finding a theme of "deflated mentality" within the girls when it came to standing firm in realizing their visions. They were keeping their dreams small because of what they were used to seeing everyday, which were successful, "finished" role models—the blogger, the thriving boss babe business, the corporate executive dressed to the nines. What wasn't readily available were the trials, tribulations, side jobs, side hustles, failures, mental anguish, or insecurities that those role models had gone through to get there. So when Kyle wanted to take this mission global and the term #GirlBoss was trending through the United States, he said to me (in true, inspirational, Kyle Wilson form) "Erika, you're working with so many of these accomplished '#Girlbosses,' it's time to re-inspire a generation, do you have a brand in mind? We're going to publish a book." I replied: "I actually do." And **Passionistas: Tips Tales and Tweetables From Women Pursuing Their Dreams** was born.

Who is the Passionista?

She is someone who translates her passion into: **Influence**, **Prosperity** and **Profound Impact**. She is WORLD-CLASS. She wears her passion on her sleeve and inspires others through her own example. She does not spend her time thinking about "what isn't going right today," but rather what is working for her and how she can utilize her resources to take massive action toward her goals. She capitalizes on her gifts—not only to design her dream life, but also to turn her interests into a fulfilling career! She transforms the old model of competition in business, to *collaboration,* and standing strong for her greatness and the greatness of others.

If you are not a passionista yet, let the stories you're about to read instruct and inspire you to make that shift. We are all behind you.

Sincerely,

Erika De La Cruz

In Front of the Curtain

By Erika De La Cruz

46 **unread messages:** I sit for a moment staring at my computer screen that has filled to the brim with greetings, tiding, stories, and congratulations. I whittled my inbox down to just four last night. I feel my left front tooth graze my bottom lip and bite down slowly as thin veils of water hydrate my eyes.

One inbound message, then another. I feel a buzzing beneath the blanket that's draped over me in the center of my couch and reach down, trying not to spill my coffee as I search for my phone. I pull it out just as the ringing stops. A family member. More missed calls. A green message icon with a tiny circle notification reading "22." I click into the first message to read "**You're on Huffington Post today girl! What is life.**"

I let a tear finally fall down my cheek accompanied by a short laugh. The laughter of familiarity and newness combined. The *familiar* part—the support of my community and peer groups…responding to something I aimed to achieve and accomplished. But, the *new* part—tears of gratitude and excitement, rather than the feeling of uncertainty. The tear falling is not so new, but the reason behind it—is freeing and beautiful.

In the past, an in-pour of support and congratulatory messages meant one thing for me—*fear*.

Through the midst of hitting my goals during college, landing my first job as the youngest ever Marketing Director at age 22 for Entercom Broadcasting and simultaneously maintaining my role as an on-air personality for Entercom's Southern California radio stations, I shared my wins with a few loved ones, a few peer groups and, of course—all of my colleagues knew as well. But every time I'd get a "way to go!" it was followed by my own thoughts screaming—*I hope they don't find out that I don't know what I'm doing.*

In the next couple years, I transitioned to television and my dream of being a late night show guest came true. My continued hustle to maintain my day job and also build my DREAM job via email reach-outs and connections led to one of my biggest goals realized: red carpet correspondence. Red carpet interviews and event run-ins came in sequence after that—Ellen Degeneres, Adrien Brody, Alan Arkin, Josh Duhamel, Beau Bridges, Demi Lovato. Casual run-ins and picking the brains of some of my FAVORITE stars became a weekly happening. I felt grateful and yet, all I could think was—*I really hope they don't peel back my curtain.* My thoughts would consume me in between takes and I'd drift off into recent memories:

> *This kind of thing doesn't happen for girls like me. If they knew my past, if they knew I was in some pain, surely they'd know I don't belong…. I'm a girl who after just one year of college, returned home to find my family broken. My house foreclosed. My new home for the following weeks—a 1993 Honda Accord where I kept all of my items. I had to move in with family friends wondering where my mom went. And wouldn't find out for a few years that she chose to retreat into homelessness, saying goodbye to society for a while. And me.*

These thoughts made me believe anything but I'm "The Real Deal." Which was what was echoed from my friends' high fives after each event. The same sentiment was mirrored by my community's "congratulations" following conversations and Instagram posts, or tweets from my accounts. I should have been exuberant… but what was present was the feeling of fraudulence. The feeling of being an outsider. The feeling that maybe my accomplishments were somehow—*fake*, or that *if anyone found out I got lucky… surely, I must be hiding something.* Am I doing this right? The support left me seeking permission. And an overwhelming feeling of responsibility would creep in as I'd question whether or not I deserved any praise.

Then, following the transition into entrepreneurship and the pursuit of my personal brand, I was asked to share my story in a "SUE Talk," the female equivalent of a TEDx in California. I was hesitant. I almost declined. I can not tell you what allowed me to write that speech, or have the courage to go and tell everyone about what I'd been through. To tell everyone that-following those other circumstances, all of the items left from my childhood were sold to the state of California. That over the period of about 3 years following, anyone could go and rummage my youth at local flea-markets, purchase a jewelry box I'd received for my 13th birthday, with my high-school sweetheart's love note still inside. That I spent the rest of college receiving Facebook messages from loved ones and strangers alike about seeing a familiar set of our furniture at a swap meet, or a frame with my picture still inside. And finally, my childhood nanny, who was actively going and retrieving these items in secret, so that she could give them back to me, actually purchased my Grandmother's urn at one of the markets. It was labeled "marble jar $3.99." I shared all of that, shared that I missed my mom every day. And then, something curious happened, I had to actually FINISH the story. "Then what happened?" and the answer was:

Then…. Well, I felt really grateful? Then…. I developed a network of friends and family who I would have never had such a bond with without these circumstances. Then I worked harder than anyone I knew to maintain my lifestyle, then I pursued my profession like a BOSS? I went from applying for scholarships with $6 in my bank account to smiling on a red carpet in the center of Los Angeles' finest venue, starting a successful brand and business…. and ultimately, cultivating some of the most precious relationships with my friends, mentors, and family that I could have ever dreamed of… I did that.

What I realized through sharing my story, was that—there was nothing behind the curtain, nothing for anyone to find out. I actually accomplished those things.

Following that SUE Talk, thousands of people were able to access my story. I was asked to speak on "personal development" stages. "Developing yourself… personally," this was a concept that rang more true than anything I'd ever done. I became the host of *Brian Tracy's Success Mastery Academy* for entrepreneurs via my new partner, Kyle Wilson, who had also watched my SUE talk and knew in that instant that up lifting other people would color the rest of my career. My brand in entertainment, coaching, and speaking is based in mindset and creating your dream life. Good *JUJU* at it's finest. Finally, I've developed a brand, book, and platform to allow other women to share their story too. It's called *Passionistas, Tips Tales and Tweetables from Women Pursuing their Dreams* and you're reading it ☺.

The Truth. The Take-Aways.

- Each time I accomplished some new goal or idea (*with certainty it was being done wrong*) each time I posted onto my social outlets (*feeling impolite*) each time I received a congratulatory message (*and felt like a fraud*) each new opportunity I took (*feeling that I got lucky*) each new relationship I cultivated (*hoping "they don't find out",*) each time I thought—*who do I think I am?*—that's how I discovered who I really was.

- Aspiring passionistas, aspiring human beings for that matter, it's supposed to feel this way. If the first bullet resonates—it's because you're up to something big, something great. Something scary and UNCERTAIN. You're fulfilling your purpose at the level your soul has required you to.

- It's supposed to feel too good to be true—until the "to good to be" dissolves and all you're left with is "*true.*" Look forward to that moment. Do NOT stop. What awaits is the realization that what inspires you most can actually become your entire life if you design it that way. Through what you have lived, you also have achieved.

As I sit on the couch, my blanket still swaddling my computer and iPhone that both set the stage for the firework display of messages coming in from my loved ones, I feel the new, content feeling cloak me: bliss and appreciation. The supportive messages are similar to before, but my brief tears emulate only gratitude. Gratitude and the belief that I am the real deal and that everyone is, really. They just have to realize it. There is nothing behind anyone's curtain.

TWEETABLE

Turn your day job into your dream job, your day dream into reality & that reality into inspiration. #Passionista #Itspossible #TheRealDeal
—Erika De la Cruz

Erika is a Television Personality, Speaker and Author. Founder of Passionistas: Tips Tales and Tweetables from Women Pursuing their Dreams *book, community and coaching. Nominated as* Woman to Watch— Leadership Division by the California State Senate. *Host of Brian Tracy's Success Mastery Academy. On-air personality and moderator for previous outlets: NBC, Fox Sports and The CW. Host of Fashion Week San Diego. Motivational Speaker in the #Girlboss and Millennial Empowerment Movement.*

LEARN MORE: Erikadelacruz.com

TWEET/IG: @_ErikaDeLaCruz

CONTACT: Erika@erikadelacruz.com

From Blogger to Influencer to Entrepreneur

By Gwen Lane

I wanted to be a cardiologist when I was five years old. I really didn't know what this meant at the time. All I knew was that my grandfather had a heart condition and this way, I would be able to help him.

I started my first business in the school bus when I was in third grade. I competed (not entirely legally) with the school's student store that sold Airheads for 50 cents. I borrowed the money from my parents to buy a big box and sold it on the bus for 25 cents. I loved making a profit but what I really loved was helping other students save money.

After studying Business Management Economics at UC Santa Cruz, I had no idea what to do. I worked in various companies and online startups in digital marketing and social media. I spent some time at an advertising agency in media planning for feature films. I even taught computer applications at the corporate level, where I would teach company employees Excel shortcuts and how to create pivot tables.

It was in 2014 that I started my blog, The LA Girl. I was working in digital marketing for an e-commerce company at the time and was looking for a creative writing outlet. I wanted to write about a topic that I was knowledgable in and passionate about. That's when I chose the subject of my hometown, Los Angeles.

When I first started my blog, I wanted to write about living in LA and things that other LA girls care about. I knew that they cared about health and fitness, work and money, and things happening in our city—the same things that mattered to me. I didn't really have a goal in mind when I started, I just kept writing. I was also sharing my adventures in LA on my social media channels and my audience kept growing. I would share my posts with my friends, family, and co-workers and that's how it started.

As my audience grew, brands reached out to me to review their products. I was offered compensation through free products and the brand would get exposure to my audience. When this started happening, I was ecstatic! First, I was happy that anyone even read my blog. Second, I was thrilled that companies were reaching out to me and giving me free stuff.

One of my favorite blogger opportunities happened six months after I started my blog when Ben & Jerry's invited me to go to Vermont and visit the factory. The trip was fully paid for and I got to visit Vermont, where I had never been before. I met other bloggers there and had a fantastic time!

Shortly after, my very first paid opportunity came. I was offered a fee to create content around a brand's product. I was very excited for this and wanted to make sure I stayed true to my authentic self and tested out the product, before recommending it to my readers.

I kept writing in my blog on a regular basis and would get paid opportunities here and there. Meanwhile, the company where I was working for my day job got acquired and closed down the LA office, so all of us were laid off. Fortunately, I got hired at an entertainment company as a Digital Marketing Manager.

I continued working on my side hustle and balanced it with my job. I would get up every morning at 6am and work on my blog and social media channels before I would go into work. I would also work during the evenings and on weekends.

As my readership and audience grew, I would receive event invites and other paid opportunities. I had reached the point where I didn't want to just receive product samples anymore. It took a lot of work to create beautiful photos, a blog post, and social media posts. I decided at that point to no longer take product samples as a form of compensation and only made a few exceptions.

It was then that my blog turned into a business and I went from blogger to influencer. I started attracting bigger brands and higher paying projects that included event hosting and promotion. I started working with brands like Verizon, Nissan, Nordstrom, Starbucks, Target, etc. It was about a year and a half after the launch of my blog that I really started thinking about doing this full time.

In the meantime, my day job was really fun. I had a great team and a boss who was flexible and knew about my side hustle. Many of my co-workers followed me on Instagram and would see the things that I would do outside of work. A lot of them would read my blog to find out about cool things to do in LA. Although I wasn't miserable at my day job, I realized that I would rather be working on building my own company. I also started feeling that I wanted to make an impact on the world. I didn't know exactly what that would look like at the time, but I knew I wasn't going to be able to do it by staying there.

I started attending blogger conferences and there I would meet other fellow bloggers. I found that a lot of them had the same questions about how to monetize their blog and social media channels and how to transition to working on it full time. It was then that I had a burning desire to provide other bloggers with this information. I had gained this knowledge throughout my blogging experience and wanted to share it others.

Through my blogging journey, I made the biggest discovery of my life. I was given the gift of knowledge and experience and it became my mission and purpose to give it back. That's where my idea for my new business, Elegant Blogger, was formed. I want to teach other bloggers and influencers how to monetize their blogs and social channels so that they too can achieve their dreams and empower others.

For a very long time, I thought that I was wandering aimlessly. It wasn't until very recently when I started doing a lot of working on myself that I realized that I wasn't. I worked in so many different places doing so many different things. Turns out, I was supposed to have all those experiences and I was supposed to learn how to do everything I know now. I was supposed to do all of it. All of my experiences have led me to this point and I am here to give it everything I've got.

TWEETABLE
When you're given the gifts of knowledge and experience, it's your mission and purpose to give it back.
—Gwen Lane @thelagirl @elegantblogger #purpose

Gwen Lane is a multi-passionate blogger, influencer, and entrepreneur. She is founder of the Los Angeles lifestyle blog, The LA Girl, which reaches millions of millennial women in Los Angeles. After creating a six-figure business from her blog just two years after launch, she created a new venture, Elegant Blogger, to help other bloggers monetize their platforms and empower them to become full-time entrepreneurs. Connect with her on Instagram via @thelagirl. Learn more at http://thelagirl.com

The Best Thing I Never Achieved

By Kathy Selim

They say that life does not give you a road map—it gives you a Mom. My mom was, and is the reason for my success. She was my number one supporter, and encouraged me to pursue my passions fearlessly. She sadly passed away in 2015 from brain cancer, but I want to share with you some of the greatest lessons I learned from her in the pursuit of my career. This is the story of the greatest thing I never achieved.

My mom was not like most moms. Ligia Selim moved to the U.S. when she was 18 years old from Bogota, Colombia. Like most immigrants she did not speak English, but that did not stop her from pursuing her dreams. She enrolled in Boston University and graduated with a degree in Fine Art. At age 25, she joined the U.S. Air Force and was stationed in London, England. By the time my mom was in her late 20s, she had traveled through most of Europe, Scandinavia, and Asia. She left the Air Force when she met my dad and settled for housewife status. But, that didn't last long! My mom wanted to find a way to help people. She knew how difficult it was to be in the U.S. and not be able to speak English. So, she decided to pursue a career as a Spanish and English interpreter. She was not successful at first, but by the time I was out of high school my mom had grown her small business into a successful interpreting agency.

When it was time for me to begin pursuing my career she insisted my education come first. My mom would say "you could lose everything, but no one can ever take away your education." Those words resonated with me, and in 2007 I applied and was accepted into the International Business program at San Diego State University. The IB program was one of the best in the nation. IB Students are part of an intense five-year program with an emphasis on business and foreign language studies. Students are required to have an internship in a foreign country for one year, and I knew I would complete my internship in Spain. I loved Europe because my mom had lived there, and I loved Spain because they spoke Spanish. That was all I needed to know to pick this major.

I succeeded in my general education and Spanish courses, however I struggled in math and business. After 3 years, my math scores were so low I was forced to change my major. Just like that, my dreams of having an internship in Spain were gone. I felt like a failure, I had set goals for myself, and I did not achieve them. The last person I wanted to tell was my mom. I finally found the courage to tell her I was going to change my major to communication. I waited until we were on vacation. I began to cry, and explained that IB was no longer for me. I could tell it was not what she had expected to hear that day. She told me that it would all work out and that communication suited my personality better anyway. As for the internship, maybe I was meant to find something closer to home. She was so supportive that I made a vow to myself that I would not fail again. I would pursue my studies with determination and focus. When I returned from vacation, I began enrolling in on-campus clubs and organizations with the intention of making school my first priority. That Spring I joined a club called (RED) to help raise awareness about the AIDS epidemic in Africa. All of our hard work led up to a (RED) Night concert at House of Blues San Diego (HOB SD).

There was a feeling that came over me that night in that small club; I was part of something bigger than myself. I felt like a part of a team that was creating a once-in-a-lifetime experience for others, and I loved that feeling.

As I hung my last poster, a woman I didn't know approached me. "Hey, how's it going?" I said.

She introduced herself, "I'm Noelle, I've been watching you, and you look like a hard worker. I wish I had more interns like you!" I had no idea who she was, but I knew I wanted an internship and this was the next step towards that goal. I gave her my email address, and she disappeared into the crowd. Looking back now, that was the night I fell in love with event planning. I had never been so happy or felt so validated than in that moment. That was the statement that solidified my career choice.

Two weeks later I received the email below:

> Hi Kathy,
>
> It was nice meeting you at the House of Blues the other night. I am looking for a new marketing intern and would like to have you come into the office for an interview. Let me know when you can stop by.
>
> Noelle
>
> House of Blues San Diego

A few weeks later, I began working in Downtown San Diego as the marketing intern for HOB. My mom was so proud of me and I had proven to myself that I could accomplish any goal I set for myself. It wasn't a glamorous Spanish internship but it was something even better. I had found my purpose. My mom believed in me when I didn't believe in myself. She inspired me to pick myself, move forward, and remain optimistic about my future.

After a semester at House of Blues, I went on to intern at Live Nation in Chula Vista, and eventually landed my first job as event coordinator in Beverly Hills. At 22, I began planning high profile events for A-list celebs. Over the last 4 years I have organized over 700 events for clients such as Match.com, Sony Pictures Classics, Kia, Pepsi and Amazon.com. These events ranged from singles mixers, North American Tours, film premieres to a Maxim Super Bowl XLIX Party. I have been lucky enough to travel to some of the most prestigious film festivals, all thanks to my job. In 2016, I became the Event and Marketing Manager for TheWrap News Inc.

What I learned from this experience is that life can be unpredictable, and that the road map to our goals is not always going to be how we envision it. We may not succeed at first, but when we make our passions our first priority, we allow for amazing opportunities to align in our life. I hope that you remember to stay optimistic and to consult your hopes and your dreams whenever you are in doubt because our perceived failures can lead us on a beautiful road to our dream job.

TWEETABLE
"When we make our passions our first priority, we allow for amazing opportunities to align in our lives."

Kathy Selim, Event & Marketing Manager for TheWrap, manages TheWrap Screening Series, pop-up interview studios, and renowned entertainment, media and tech conference TheGrill. Kathy was the youngest Match.com event planner at A-list Communications and first planner for Match.com Canada, has traveled North America planning high-profile events for A-list celebrities, and was assistant producer for Maxim Super Bowl Party XLIX. She mentors and encourages young ladies to pursue their dreams.

Twitter @lovekathy

Instagram @lovekathyxo

Chores, Choices & Ralph Lauren

By Hillary Gadsby

I always had the entrepreneurial bug. In fact, I attribute the success I have to hard work and being able to cultivate relationships. I did not come from a wealthy family, but I learned early on that creating and building relationships are the building blocks of any business. It is important to start building valuable relationships at a young age because we never know what those relationships will forge in the future.

At 10 years old, I had no idea what an entrepreneur was, but I knew that I didn't want to depend on my parents for money. It wasn't about having my own business; it was about being able to afford the things that I wanted on my own. I started to babysit some neighborhood kids every weekend. The typical rate in my hometown was $20/hour. I knew that this kind of money was going to help me on my path to whatever I wanted. As the weekends passed by I kept getting referrals to work for other families. It got to the point where I could no longer do this alone, so I recruited two of my girlfriends to help me out with the other families. I charged the original $20 per hour and they made $15 an hour. I pocketed the extra $10 an hour from both of them.

Now, I know some people might ask, "How is babysitting the start of an entrepreneurial journey?" What's important is the lesson that I learned while doing it. I built connections, got referred to more and more families, and this started my understanding of the power of relationships.

When I was 15, I was offered a lucrative retail position in the Sun Valley ski resort. I was in the big leagues now, selling luxury brands like Ralph Lauren. I always loved the brand and coveted that little polo pony on the shirts. One day, my mom walked into the store with a gentleman whom I had never met before. He was an old family friend, and they'd happened to run into each other outside. Little did I know, my entire life would change in that very instant.

The gentleman happened to be one of the most prominent businessmen in Las Vegas. He was very nice and asked me if I liked working with the Ralph Lauren brand. Of course, I nodded and gave a big grin. He told me that Ralph Lauren was a good friend of his and if I ever wanted to work for the company, I should give him a call.

Fast forward to my first year of college. I was sitting in my dorm room doing my homework when I received a call from my mom that would change the course of my life. She had an opportunity for me to move to Paris and become a jeune fille au pair (a live-in nanny) for her friend's 9-year-old daughter. My mom has always been great at building relationships and manifesting unique opportunities. This was an example of that. I will always be grateful for her influence and guidance and how it has shaped me throughout my life.

At 19 years of age, I hopped on a plane to Paris to live for a year with a family that I didn't know. I studied French for about 8 years prior. But, one cannot truly learn a language until he or she is immersed into speaking it daily. It turned out, unbeknownst to me, the family I was working for was extremely prominent. While I was living there, the lady of the house won the prestigious Legion D'Honneur, an honorable award given out by the President of France, who at the time was Jacques Chiraq. Today she is the 60th most powerful woman in the world as listed by Fortune Magazine. While I was working there, she quickly became my mentor. She taught me poise, confidence, and communication skills. I would not be where I am today without the lessons that she taught me.

At the end of my stay in Paris, I realized that I didn't want to return to the United States. I applied to The American University of Paris to get a BA in International Business. One of my marketing classes asked me to do a thesis on a well-known brand, so I decided to pick my favorite one, Ralph Lauren. I decided to contact the gentleman I had met a few years prior. He told me he would be happy to help and that he would put me in touch with the Paris office.

My thesis received rave reviews from the professor and my class. Shortly after, I contacted the gentleman once again to inquire about an internship with Ralph Lauren. The very next day, I received a call from Ralph Lauren's son, who informed me that he set up an interview for me with human resources in Paris. I went to the interview and was hired for a yearlong internship in the marketing department in Paris.

Today, I have built a community of female entrepreneurs and business leaders that continues to grow. I have inspired, educated, and connected many young women all across the country through my company, Stiletto Gal. I use the relationships that I have carefully built since my first entrepreneurial experience babysitting at 10 years old to help others in their own journey.

I cannot stress enough how important it is to start making your connections early. Each of these stories illustrates the value of how powerful it is to take risks, be courageous, and nurture relationships. The people you meet, be they mentors, friends, or even future bosses, will be valuable to you on your career path. Remember, it's not only what you know—who you know is equally important.

TWEETABLE

It's not only what you know; it's who you know that is equally important
—Hillary Gadbsy #stilettogalboss #weinspire #passionistas

As Founder of A Gadsby Affair, Hillary Gadsby's ability to put her clients in the public eye has gained her recognition among brands such as Ralph Lauren, Gucci and Vera Wang. As Founder & Chief Visionary Officer of Stilettogal.com, she inspires and connects future female business leaders.

Nominated as woman to watch at 2016 Women of Influence Awards & Business Owner of the Year at 2016 LA Business Journal Women's Summit.

www.stilettogal.com

Forbes Spotlight: http://tinyurl.com/forbeshillarygadsby

Cookie and the Creams: My Journey to Self Love

By Krystal Aaron

As if, whatever, get the picture, duh. These aren't words you typically expect to hear from a young black girl's mouth. But, as the "cookie" amongst "creams" in Rancho Cucamonga, CA it was practically inevitable for me to adapt.

Rancho's Black population was barely 5% throughout my childhood. From the people I saw on a daily basis I'm surprised it was even that high. Needless to say, I was different. Being apart of the 5% was lonely and I hated it, but I felt a responsibility to be grateful for the opportunity. My West Indian parents immigrated to the United States and worked hard for this lifestyle. They were proud of their Corporate America jobs and two-story house; so how selfish was I to complain about living the "American Dream?" A part of me was proud of what my parents had become. I loved having my own room and being able to travel the world at a young age, but I didn't fit in. I wasn't like the other children I spent six hours with everyday at school; we lived what seemed to be two different lives. We didn't eat the same foods, we didn't have the same rules at home, and our physical features were polar opposites. I spent all day feeling like an outsider looking in and it took a major toll on my self esteem.

So how does a five-year-old black girl survive in a predominantly white elementary school? Duh—she becomes Beyoncé and tells everyone to "Bow Down," an icon and queen in her own right. At least, that's how I wish I handled it. Instead my youth was spent in a series of confusion and mental turmoil. Being the child performer that I was, I would adopt several characters for myself. I ended up juggling twelve different personalities at the same time. I went from sporty to girly to nerdy to just straight up weird in one recess in an effort to find my place in the social circle of elementary school.

By the time I got to the twelfth version of myself, I was lonelier than ever. I was this overly involved, hyper, social butterfly that could float from group to group, but still I felt as though I didn't belong. You see, by not being my true self, I created a false sense of relationships with superficial connections to people I barely knew, who barely knew me.

When I started to feel like I got a handle on elementary school, it was time for junior high. Junior high integrated all of Rancho's elementary schools, meaning I was about to be surrounded by more of the 5%! Finally, people who understand me. WRONG. The rest of the 5% had already been around each other and formed a tight clique that had no room for me. I was still different because now I was the true cookie. Oh yes, the Oreo cookie who is black on the outside and white on the inside. And they never let me forget it. I tried to find my place by joining multiple extracurricular activities, but instead I felt alone in a crowded room with more superficial relationships. High school was just like junior high and the cycle seemed unbreakable. But then, it was time for college.

YAY! A completely fresh start. I wasn't the Oreo or the black girl, I was Krystal, and I was ready to take on campus as me. Uh oh! I don't know who I am! I've been juggling so many personalities, how do I be me? Well, one thing I knew for sure was what I looked like, so I immediately joined Black Student Union. There was no way I was going to be the Oreo all over again. I surrounded myself with the Black community on campus, joining the most prestigious black sorority and I later became the President of our BSU. I met people from all over the world and had unforgettable moments, but I still wasn't happy. I was living in a city people dream of merely visiting, going to a college full of opportunities, and had amazing friends and family; yet I still felt like an outsider. How could I be so ungrateful, how could I be so lonely?

That was when I finally snapped. Second semester of my sophomore year I made a decision that would change my life: I decided I wanted to kill myself. Now we won't go into my obviously failed attempt at suicide, but I ended up spending that night in a mental institution. It was a state facility mental institution, not the fancy ones suburban princesses on television shows go to. It was the real deal, rock bottom type of facility. 24 hours earlier I was in class as a private school accounting student, and now I was surrounded by homeless drug addicts and sleeping on a cold tile floor. This was not what my parents had in mind when they sent me away to college. What have I done? Am I really this broken? And what the hell am I going to do now?

The next morning the lead psychiatrist pulled me into a room and asked me a series of questions. I answered the questions perfectly so I would be released. Luckily, it worked. I walked out of the mental institution to find my mother and sister waiting for me. I was so relieved to see them, but I was ashamed of my actions. I couldn't continue pretending anymore, there's only one Krystal so I took the semester off to find her.

This was the hardest thing I ever had to do. I had been so used to being other people for years and years that the "real me" was completely foreign. It took me a long time to escape this mental frenzy and to say I fully have today would be a lie. I have numerous talents, as many of us do, but loving myself has never come naturally. Nevertheless, it is the most important thing I have worked towards. So, I began searching for myself and slowly finding her.

Through finding myself I learned my power as a woman, we are a strong species and there's nothing we can't do. But, we have to start with self-love. Rihanna once said, "The minute you learn to love yourself you would not want to be anybody else." Once I started to discover my gifts and value myself I could drop those twelve personalities and be one dynamic person. I don't need to fit into a group because being different is the best part about me. We are all different. We each have something that makes us stand out and that's how we leave our mark on this world. Each of us has something another person can use, and if we work together as women we can combine our strengths to help each other. Today, I am on a mission to empower an army of women who will work together to achieve their dreams through my new community, Klassy Verre. I am happy to say women have been inspired to not only achieve the impossible, but have formed genuine connections with women who support them despite their differences.

Currently, I take daily steps towards self-mastery and it has greatly improved all aspects of my life. It's an ongoing process, but I encourage you start NOW. This is how I began that transformation:

First, try to remain in a constant state of gratitude. For example, instead of hating your hair for not achieving the perfect messy bun, switch to a positive thought about your tresses or immediately celebrate another feature. You must learn to celebrate the little things to be at peace with what you think are your flaws.

Next, remind yourself that you are a Queen, Goddess, Bombshell, Badass, Passionista taking over the world. You can do this by saying positive daily affirmations in the morning like, "I am unique and the world needs me to be the best version of myself." Always avoid comparing yourself to others; you can say "I am grateful for my life and my uniqueness is my gift." Feel free to say more affirmations throughout the day.

Lastly, actively become the person you want to be. We all have a dream version of ourselves and we get there through choices and actions we make today. Approach situations as though you already are who you want to be and eventually you will become her.

RECAP:
1. Stay in a constant state of gratitude
2. Say daily affirmations
3. Be your dream self

With these three steps you can drastically improve your life and obtain self-mastery. Who better to become acquainted with than yourself right? It may not come easy, or quickly, but it will be worth it.

I made the mistake of hiding my uniqueness and authenticity and it drove me into a mental institution. It wasn't until I learned to embrace myself that I began creating my dream life. Take control of your life and start embracing what makes you different. Then use it to conquer the world.

TWEETABLE

No matter who says they love you, who likes your photos, or who pays you, nothing will matter until you learn to love yourself #passionistas

Krystal Aaron is a Disney lover and feminist who believes women are stronger in numbers. After obtaining her Accounting Degree, Krystal began pursuing her passion for empowering women. She developed an emerging online and in person community for glamorous and ambitious women called Klassy Verre. With already two successful events, Klassy Verre creates a positive atmosphere for like-minded millennial women to learn and connect. Connect with Krystal on Instagram at @krystal_aaron or check out her community of female goal crushers at klassyverre.com

Turning Teens into Tycoons

By Olenka Cullinan

"Here you go, Miss!"
This boy comes up to me and gives me a note
when I stop speaking.
"What is this?" I say,
"You. Are. Beautiful!" he says.
"It's my suicide note," he says,
"But I'm going to be ok now."

— From "My Dear Student" poem by Olenka Cullinan

The teen walked away from the room without ever turning back. I stood there flabbergasted, teary-eyed, with my hands and lips quivering simultaneously, and my mind in disarray thinking of what to do with this note. I watched his straight back and saw release in his shoulders, and I knew inside the depth of my aching heart that he was, really, going to be ok. I came to that small town Iowa school to speak as an international college student to inspire teens "just for fun." When I left, I had realized two things—I connected with teens' souls and working with youth was my life's journey.

Defying the expectation my mother had for me to take over her CEO position in the factory she built, at age 20, after the most drawn out and devastating divorce between my parents, I moved to the US with $450 in my pocket. While I grew up in a fairly well-to-do family, by 16 I went through a reversed princess syndrome when my dad started drinking heavily and sold most of our belongings for booze. I was a daddy's girl until I was 12, and I was passionate about education since I was 5. I still remember playing school with my dolls and assigning school roles to all family members. I loved my Granpa the most, so he was the principal. Professionally, we had no teachers or counselors in my family.

Watching my mother, a die-hard-entrepreneur, go out on a limb every day of her existence taught me that anything could be made possible. Since I was little, she would say, "Whatever you will, happens." I always wondered if borrowing $450 from my uncle and moving to another country was willful enough by her standards.

My college years weren't particularly easy, since regardless of my hard work, and making Dean's List every semester, I was a foreigner with no ability to receive any type of aid or scholarships. Working 3 jobs just to pay for my private college and basic existence was never my idea of fun. I remember vividly living off one bag of chips for about 3 days. I also remember how my roommate and I broke into a hysterical laughter when my mother, who was visiting at a time, offered to make us an omelette. Poor woman did not know that we were worried about turning into chickens since we'd been eating mostly eggs for about 2 months prior to her arrival.

Having made it onto a debate team and being lucky enough to have had professors who always put students first, I finally zeroed in on my dream—to teach college. I became quite proficient in slam poetry and always loved being in the youth environment; I had taken more psychology classes than most counselors due to my Russian university degree. Then the unthinkable happened—there were no higher education jobs in Phoenix. Not willing to give up on teaching as a career path, I enlisted myself into a last resort inner city school in Phoenix as an English teacher. At the moment, I didn't realize that I would be building my own version of "Freedom Writers" which was going to manifest itself as Rising Tycoons, the course I would use to help more than 6,000 students around the world and that I would present on TEDx Live.

I knew with certainty that reading classics with these students might prove challenging. I did know that this was a school full of possibilities. It was a school full of students whom society saw as flawed, but who I saw as broken, as teens who were like me—starting without much, without resources, without family support, many as immigrants from another country.

My very first day I had to borrow a dry erase marker next door, after a maybe 2 minute absence, I saw a group of angel-looking students, sitting at their desks with arms crossed neatly at their desks. Then, I looked on the whiteboard—it was splattered with blood. No other signs of any kind of altercation made it clear for me. Never leave the classroom without supervision again.

My second week of teaching, I was looking in the eyes of a 17-year old boy who had recited Shakespeare in my classroom that morning, while I was signing off as a character witness for his deposition case for rape that afternoon. I knew that I had to push these students outside of the classroom walls and boxed mentality to change their lives.

It was one of the most challenging, fun-filled, life-lived years of my life. It made me realize that I carried the reasons all of these students said they couldn't be successful—I was an immigrant, I moved to the US with $450 in my pocket, I had an accent, I started with no resources, and I had no support system except for the kind strangers whom I met along the way. Countless people who had driven me to Goodwill for household items, who donated clothes and even paid for some of my college. People, many of whom became life-long friends, and mentored me into success. I realized that most of these students were creating shadows by standing in their own sunshine because no one was there to teach them to move differently, to think differently, to abandon the box mentality.

I was hired out of that school by an early college high school within a community college system, where I was able to work further on building Backbone of Success™. I worked with many teens and parents and realized that most youth saw success as the magical unicorn, something you established if you had superpowers or were born into a family of Rockefellers. They didn't see the clear connection to failure and grind and perseverance, nor did they realize the passionate, but arduous journey between Steve Job's garage and the multimillion brand that Apple became today. For the most part, teens were taught what to think instead of "how to" think and were guided by cubicle mentality or staying in the safe, inside the box zone. I realized that it was the mindset of possibility given to me by my parents and early mentors that propelled me to create the life I have today. I learned that it takes courage to see the world not how it is, but how it should be. People who can do this can accomplish the unimaginable!

Luckily, my mother taught me to always go after "the biggest person in the room" and think like there was no box. I became relentless in seeking out the masters to help me further discern small, simple, and manageable success-building steps for teens. After training under the absolute "Yodas" of success and leadership and some of the top speakers in the country, such as John Maxwell, Andy Andrews, Josh Shipp and Darren Hardy, I strongly believe that pursuing success with happiness creates goals, vision, and destination for the youth.

Working with parents, educators and teens for over 10 years, I learned that there's an art to raising a teen tycoon. It's a process, consisting of steps, just as if we are teaching them basketball or gymnastics. A combination of three essential skills: leadership, entrepreneurship and personal development turns teens into mindful tycoons! Entrepreneurship has always been dear to my heart because it erases all barriers to success. It allows people to design a life regardless of the circumstances: the zip code they were born into, their skin color, or their gender. However, teenagers are not adults and their mindset often holds them back. Thus, I knew that Rising Tycoons programs had to initially teach personal development skills and teach teens to become CEOs of their lives.

To date, I have been able to deliver Rising Tycoons programs to teens and adult influencers from different schools, different socio-economic statuses, different cultures and have worked with many top Leadership/ Entrepreneurship organizations in the Nation: DECA, National Association of High School Principals, National Honor Society, National Association of Student Councils, Job Corps, Boys & Girls Clubs, & TEDx.

The goal is always the same—to take GenZ or millennial youth on a success journey, step by step and to teach adult influencers what it takes to raise 21st century leaders. It's nothing short of amazing to see 14-16-18 year olds abandoning the cubicle mentality, announcing themselves as CEOs of their life, launching their business ventures and turning into leaders in school, life and community. Hundreds and thousands of emails, hugs and tears later, I've been honored enough to be called anything from "teen queen," a "total badass," Olenka- lei (which stand for "Leader, Entrepreneur, and Inspiration") to "Nanny 911 but for teens." I'm a girl from a small town Russia and I've heard teens say to me that I touched their lives, that I've changed their trajectory for the future and that I gave them hope.

Outside of being a girl-boss, I like to refer to myself as "Hope and Possibility Agent." When I leave the room, I want those two feelings to linger behind within my audience. No amount of money, fame or recognition for me will ever beat doing that. My work with youth from 21 countries through some incredible partnerships combined with a touch of humor and my personal experience has made me realize how often adults set up the end result without teaching youth the "how to" process. But, just like the saying goes, "'how' is more important than 'what.'"

During one of my first workshops, I vividly remember saying to Darren Hardy, at that time still Publisher of Success magazine, and consultant to the top CEOs in the country, "I want to be just like you, but for teens!" To date, in its rather young existence, Rising Tycoons has touched the lives of over 6,000 teens in addition to their adult influencers nationwide & globally via keynotes, workshops and conferences. I have seen happy smiles of parents whose student now is "ready to be seen," I have seen teen's eyes light up because they now realize that math is connected to business plans, and I have see teachers excited because they are now inspired to bring specific hands-on entrepreneurial and leadership steps into the classroom. I have read many notes from administrators and organizers saying that I "connected the dots to success" for their youth.

My continuing question is always: how can I and Rising Tycoons programs touch more lives in a most authentic, meaningful, and real-world way? How can I inspire youth into action? The newest achievement, Rising Tycoons Academy (RTA), now available nationwide, offers hands-on, real-world training in "how to start a business," preparing a new generation of aspiring values-based entrepreneurial leaders. Its mission, to bring the real world into the classroom, came from the outcry from schools and educators for collaboration between business community and education, for teaching real leadership and entrepreneurship, and for 21st century leadership skills. I'm the prime example of what entrepreneurship, leadership and personal development can do for a young life. I understand the value of the right mentors and the power of community support and stepping outside of boxes and walls. These breed success!

In 2015, I had the honor of being invited to speak at TEDx Youth. Walking on stage in front of the audience of 750 youth and adults while blinded by lights and being live-streamed in 30 countries felt beyond what words can describe. Standing on that "X", brought memories of my first speeches practicing into hairbrush as a microphone, of my college life in a Goodwill-furnished apartment, of countless small and large failures during the birth of my business, and of the lit up eyes of the first group of teens who had the courage to call themselves and the company–Rising Tycoons. At that very moment, when the 12 minutes went by like 3, I couldn't even see the audience. But behind the dark crowd, I saw the eyes of hundreds of teens and who inspired me to get out of bed, stay in bad hotels, and drive cross country because their lives and futures matter. Rising Tycoons' tribe of teens and adults, allowed me to have hope and possibility for my life, to stand for what I believe is the pathway to the success for the future generation–turning teens into mindful tycoons.

TWEETABLE

If skills are learnable, success is learnable too! #risingtycoons #savingteensfromcubicles #passionista

Olenka Cullinan is an inspirational and TEDx speaker, Founder of Rising Tycoons, Entreprenista and GenZ & Millennial Success trainer for adult influencers. Olenka's newest achievement is Rising Tycoons Academy (RTA) launching nationwide. RTA offers hands-on, real-world of "how to start a business," preparing a new generation of aspiring values-based entrepreneurial Leaders.

Connect olenka@risingtycoons.com or

Twitter/Instagram: @olenkacullinan and @risingtycoons

Learn more: www.risingtycoons.com

Abandoned by My Parents to Passionista!

By Stefanie Overturf

Have you ever felt as though time has stopped? Those moments of glancing around and not remembering how you got to where you were going?

When I was about 14 years old I remember rapidly pedaling my bike like crazy, heading back to my grandparents' home. I had spent the last three hours at my friend's house, when I realized the time and decided to leave. There I was, riding my bike down the long road home. There was no one around, no cars going by. At that moment, time stopped for me. I remember thinking, "There is not a person in the world right now that cares where I am or what I am doing." This is not a concern one would typically attribute to a 14-year-old girl.

I had moved in with my paternal grandparents about three months prior, after realizing that my mom would continue to choose men, drugs, and partying over her own children. My dad was not in a position to raise my sisters and me either because he too had an alcohol problem. My early years were made up of moving around from one house to another and my parents moving from job to job, until they finally divorced when I was 10 years old.

It was difficult as a teenager to be in that situation and to feel that I had no control over my life. My parents' choices had created circumstances and hurdles that I would have to overcome in order to take back control of my life.

My grandparents provided a stable, safe environment, but life there was far from perfect. To this day, they are involved in a high control religion, within which every aspect of a member's life is controlled by what the leaders of the religion deem acceptable. Who you are friends with, who you marry, what your career is.

I went along with the religion for many years because it made my grandparents and the people of the church happy. But, doing this made me unhappy and it led me to suppress my true self and personal goals.

Growing up in that environment, I would never have pictured myself growing into the passionista I am today. A passionista is someone who doesn't allow unfair circumstances and/or hurdles to block her dreams and goals. Living as a passionista goes deeper than just having a career or going to work everyday. Passionistas allow their dreams to set their souls on fire and they use this to fuel their daily living. They are consumed by not just a career, but also passions. This is not the kind of thinking I was taught through the church or witnessed in my family.

Gaining this perspective was a journey and, looking back, I know it started that day on my bike. Little did I know then, that day would represent my pathway to freedom.

With my parents not around and the control of the religion surrounding me, I felt free when I was able to hop on my bike and ride. With the wind blowing against my face it seemed like my worries were gone. I wish I could've told my 14-year-old self that my freedom would one day exist beyond my solo bike rides.

It took me quite a few years to get out of the religion, but I did get out. The effects of leaving, coupled with my childhood, still affect me today. I fight low self-esteem, negative thinking and self doubt. In addition to those inner feelings, I battle the emotions that come with no longer having communication with my family and childhood friends who, due to the religion, have cut off contact with me.

My journey towards living an independent, passion-filled life began once I realized that I was responsible for my happiness and I could make a change. No matter what choices my parents made or what type of religion I was raised in, I was responsible for what I became. I started setting goals for myself personally and professionally. I began reading and listening to books that helped me see the power of my self-talk. In addition, I attended conferences that helped me develop into a leader and started sharing my story.

With the help of inspirational speakers, I've been able to get to a place where I am truly happy. Their words have impacted my life by motivating me to take control. My personal favorite Zig Ziglar says, "It's not what happens to you that determines how far you will go in life; but rather it is how you handle what happens to you." Those words have helped me realize that it's up to me to choose freedom and happiness.

In 2008 I was laid off from my corporate job and it was a scary, emotionally draining time. I didn't know what I was going to do. Again, it was one of those situations in life where I could let an external situation affect my internal feeling. Instead, I decided I was going to "ride my bike" so to speak. I would let freedom fuel my courage to control my future and financial security. I decided to start my own cleaning business.

Today, my business is the premier floor & fabric cleaning company in Southwest Florida. We have amazing employees and work for terrific clients. Overcoming those situations helped me find a career I am passionate about. And, it has helped me discover a passion for teaching others, especially young girls and women who are going through or coming out of challenging situations, to reach their full potential and become passionistas themselves.

The first time I was asked to speak publicly, self doubt reared its ugly head. I thought, "Who wants to hear from me? But, when a young lady came up to me after my speech and shared her story and how much she appreciated hearing mine, I knew I had found what I was meant to do.

I had the opportunity to speak to a graduating class of young ladies and share my story with them. One of the main things I spoke about was the fact that they don't have to stay in a rut or follow the same path that their parents did. They can break the cycle, like I did, and choose a different destiny. Knowing that someone else can benefit from my experience has motivated me to keep speaking and telling my story.

I realize now that, when I was riding my bike that day, I felt so low because I had no hope. That was a crucial time in my life when I needed to learn how to deal with those negative feelings. I really needed the help of "the good, the clean, the pure, the powerful and the positive" to quote Zig.

Today, I am a more determined, positive, and motivated person. I'm passionate about life, business and helping others. The beautiful thing about life is that we can make it whatever we want. If we're in a situation that we don't like, we can change it. If you live somewhere you don't like, move. If you are in a career that you don't love, change jobs.

I don't view challenges from a negative perspective anymore. I view them as an opportunity to get on my bike and pedal like crazy. The fact is that we will all face challenges in life. It is the universe's way of testing us before sending something huge our way. Will you be ready?

TWEETABLE

Challenges are the Universe's way of testing you before sending something huge your way...will you be ready? #willyoubeready #passionistas

Stefanie Overturf is an entrepreneur-ess, speaker, and author. She has been named an SRQ Magazine "Woman in Business," a Business Observer "40 under 40" of the brightest young stars of the business community on the Gulf Coast, and her company has been named "Small Business of the Year." She has a passion for marketing and building relationships.

To hear more, please visit www.stefanieoverturf.com

Twitter: @chicamarie83

Facebook: Facebook.com/Stefanie-Overturf

Info@stefanieoverturf.com

Brand Like A BOSS

By Devona Stimpson

I've always had a little bit of the entrepreneurial kool-aid running through me. I used to gather my neighborhood girlfriends to run a lemonade and brownie stand when I was 7 or 8 years old. We'd set it up on the street corner, screaming and hollering at every car that drove by to ask if they wanted to buy a cup of lemonade with a brownie on the side (talk about an upsell, right?). This continued throughout my days of selling stickers and toys to 4th grade classmates and running like a madwoman to start the wave in crowds at professional baseball games with friends.

All of those actions took leadership, fearlessness, persistence, and a lot of I-don't-give-a-f**k-what-you-think-about-me attitude to get the job done, which is almost everything you need to be a successful entrepreneur. These experiences served me well as I got older, but the one important thing I was missing that I learned later on was branding.

It wasn't until I gained my experience as a creative entrepreneur, that I really learned the true importance of branding. After creating my first website in the fourth grade, I began to build a career as a graphic and web designer at a very young age. I did everything from creating and selling dope MySpace layouts for friends, to creating a freelance business throughout grade school, to becoming a fine artist and selling original artworks, prints, and merchandise online.

I learned that branding isn't just your logo or your website. Branding is the perception in the consumer's mind. It's how you make people feel. It's what people think and say about you when you're not in the room. Branding is more about emotions, thoughts, and feelings than it is about conversions and transactions. You want people to miss you when you're gone, rave about you to their friends and family, and choose you over your competitors. It's an intangible asset that's the MOST important to your business.

My husband Kevin and I created a successful Branding & Creative Boutique called Strive & Grind that helps entrepreneurs create memorable, disruptive, and badass brands. Within 12 months of launching the boutique, we've worked with 20 companies and generated 6 figures in revenue which allowed us to quit our day jobs and go full-time with Strive & Grind. I want to share with you 3 impactful tips that contributed to my success while on my entrepreneurial journey.

Tip #1: Brand for Where You Want to Be, not for Where You Are Today.

Everyone has to start somewhere. But who says you have to show up like an amateur? If you want to make some real dough, you have to come out the gate with the confidence and catwalk of Beyoncé and throw the hand-made mixtapes in the trash. Branding takes the phrase "Fake it 'til you make it" and truly turns it to reality. Now, this phrase only should be applied if you have the talent and quality to back it up. Everyone can smell a shitty product or service behind a layer of makeup and perfume. At Strive & Grind, we pride ourselves on branding our clients for where they see themselves in the next 2-5 years, not for where they are today. If you want to sell products and services at a premium price, you need to make sure you look, feel, and play the part. This means all of your branding touchpoints (website, logo, email marketing, social media, customer service, storefront, uniforms, photos, packaging, and more) should be designed well, be of high quality, and give off the perception you want your customers to think and feel.

Tip #2: Invest in Your Business and Your Brand.

In March 2015, we moved from the east coast to San Diego, CA, the ultimate hub for entrepreneurship. Kevin and I went to an amazing conference that changed our lives and business forever and it was there that we hired our first business coach. We were broke, tired, frustrated, and everything in-between trying to figure out everything on our own. So our crazy asses did the unimaginable and invested over $36,000 in a coach and mastermind with no money and a lot of hope. The craziest thing is, we don't regret spending a single penny. It was his expertise and access to his mastermind that allowed us to build relationships, gain clients, grow our business, and focus on what worked best for us. Hiring a coach gave us clarity, accountability, and a huge support system like we never experienced before. Even when it came to our branding, we always made sure we invested in HIGH QUALITY web design, graphic design, video, t-shirts, packaging, stickers, wristbands, employees and everything else. We wouldn't have gotten to where we are today if we never invested that much time and money. Most people care more about making the quick buck, throwing something quickly together, and figuring everything out on their own. As a result, they end up putting their branding and business growth on the backburner and failing in the long run. It's investments in your business and branding (like the ones we made) that get you the furthest, fastest. Don't have the money? Ask your friends, aunts, grannies, moms, and dads, or get credit cards. That's what we did! It's all a mindset. You gotta ask yourself, "How bad do I want it?"

Tip #3: Be Memorable, Disruptive, and Badass (MDB)!

What do Beyoncé and Apple have in common? They're both MDB: Memorable, Disruptive, and Badass! No one else secretly drops an album or performs the way Beyoncé does and no one else creates and launches a beautiful product the way Apple does. For Strive & Grind, no one else offers a full branding experience to their clients the way we do or designs, creates, or dresses as well as we do. All of these things are elements that make us all MDB. Stop worrying about and modeling after what everyone else is doing. Ask yourself, "How can I stand out? What can I do different?" What would I want someone else to do for me that no one else is doing?" Maybe you celebrate your clients by putting them in a 5-star hotel with spa credit, maybe you play Biggie or Baltimore Club music at your events, or maybe you put a surprise gift in the packages you send to your customers. Being MDB is the best and fastest way to make more money, build brand loyalty, and create a tribe of raving fans.

Overall, being an entrepreneur is fun, hard, excruciating, exhausting, exciting, amazing, and everything in-between. If you don't invest time, patience, hustle, and money into your brand, your business, and yourself, all you'll have is a cool idea that no one will know about. If you keep Strivin' & Grindin' and focus on the 3 tips above, you'll be on your way to becoming one badass passionista!

TWEETABLE

Brand for where you want to be, not for where you are today. #strivengrind #passionista #girlboss

Devona Stimpson is the Co-Founder of Strive & Grind, a Branding & Creative Boutique, where she helps entrepreneurs create memorable, disruptive, and badass brands. She is also the Fine Artist and Designer behind DevonaStimpson.com.

Connect at DevonaStimpson.com, STRIVENGRIND.com, or email devona@strivengrind. com. Instagram: @_DEVONA_, Facebook & Snapchat: @devonastimpson

Romantic Relationships: The Power to Derail You or Propel You Forward on Your Path to Success

By Heidi Rauld

If you're a passionista, no doubt you've had the concept of the power of professional relationships drilled into your head—the importance of networking, mentors, and great partnerships. What about romantic relationships? Do they play a role in determining your future success? The answer is a resounding YES! Yet, you certainly won't find any books titled "Dating for Career Success," while perusing the business section of your local bookstore. The fact is romantic relationships have immense power to impact your career for better or worse.

At this point you might be saying to yourself, "Hold on, you can't expect to have a successful romantic relationship and be successful in business too, can you?" Well, I'm here to tell you not only can you have success in both arenas, but a successful romantic relationship can be just the right catalyst for your career success.

Romantic relationships have the power to either derail you from the path to achieving your personal and professional goals or to lift you to new heights and put you on the fast track to success. This, my fellow passionistas, is a painful lesson I had to learn and one I hope you can avoid learning firsthand by heeding my advice.

Being a passionista by definition means you are one passionate woman, right? Right! However, sometimes our passions, when misdirected, get us into trouble in the romance department.

One of my greatest passions has always been caring for people in need, which was awesome in many respects, but not so great when it came to the romance department. I had the tendency to choose men who were "projects." You know the type… men who had a few great qualities but were also in need of a major life overhaul.

As a result, I wasted years of my twenties, attempting (unsuccessfully, I might add) to help these men achieve their potential or trying to save relationships, which were doomed from day one. Instead of focusing solely on my goals, I allowed my poor relationship choices to consume my time and energy, leaving little of those precious resources to devote to my own personal growth and ambitions.

Before I realized what happened, I sacrificed many of my own dreams and stalled my career growth. Bottom line is this: bad relationships have the ability to drag you down into a muddy pit, where your partner's issues become yours. You can waste months or even years before climbing out of that pit, muddy and bruised with a perplexed expression wondering... what the heck happened? I've seen this happen to several strong, successful women. Many of these women had enough sense and determination to climb out of the pit, but some got stuck there indefinitely.

Of course, the best way to avoid getting stuck is to steer clear of the pit to begin with, which brings me to the other side of the coin. On the flipside, a great relationship can propel you forward towards your goals faster than you ever thought possible. I know this to be true because over the past few years I've been fortunate enough to experience this type of relationship.

After recognizing and changing my relationship patterns I looked for a partner who would not only support and encourage my ambitions but also be actively working toward goals of his own. If I didn't find those qualities in a man, then I was determined to remain single rather than repeat my past mistakes. Thankfully, I found (and married) a wonderful man, who is supportive of my goals and who not only is my partner in life but in business as well. Together, we help each other reach new heights and succeed in every area of life.

But, don't just take my word for it. Recently, a study from Washington University in St. Louis found that your spouse's personality significantly influences your career success. In other words, the spouse or partner you choose has a direct effect on the level of success you'll achieve over your lifetime. So ladies, you better choose wisely! With decisions such as this, you need to utilize both your head and your heart.

How do you know if you're in a relationship that has the potential to knock you off track? Here are some questions to ask yourself to help you determine if you're being derailed by your relationship.

Does your partner have a negative view on life and the world?

Is your partner only interested in how your passions, skills, and talents can help him?

Does your partner discourage you from pursuing your dreams and passions?

Is your partner controlling and places demands on your time?

Do you find your energy is drained after spending time with him?

If you've answered yes to any of these questions then I'd say it's time for you to reevaluate your relationship.

Or maybe the relationship isn't bad or unhealthy, so to speak, but it isn't necessarily positive either. You might be passionate about him, but find you've left little time or energy for pursuing your passions. In such cases, you might need to take a step back and make sure you're truly happy with where you're allocating your most precious resources: your time, brain power, energy and focus.

If you're currently single or realizing you need to make a relationship change, here are some qualities you'll want to look for in a relationship to ensure your partner will help and not hinder your path to success:

Look for a partner who...

> *...has a positive outlook on life.*

> *...is actively working towards his/her goals.*

> *...encourages you to pursue your dreams and goals.*

> *...strives for continued personal growth in all aspects of life and business.*

> *...is conscientious.*

This last point may seem odd at first glance, but researchers with the Washington University in St. Louis study found workers with the highest levels of success had spouses who scored high for conscientiousness in personality tests.

Furthermore, in the book The Millionaire Mind, author Thomas J. Stanley devotes an entire chapter to the qualities millionaires' spouses possess and how these qualities contribute to their success. He found the top five qualities millionaires' spouses possessed were: honest, responsible, loving, capable, and supportive. Therefore, if you'd like to eventually become a millionaire, these might be a few more qualities to look for in a potential partner.

Passionistas, take advice from someone who knows, and don't allow a bad relationship to keep you from reaching your highest potential and becoming the rockstar you are meant to be! Make wise relationship decisions now, and you'll reap the rewards in every area of life for years to come.

TWEETABLE

Romantic relationships have power; bad ones will derail you, great ones will propel you on the path to success.
—Heidi Rauld #passionistas

Heidi Rauld is a wife, mother, marketer, entrepreneur, and photographer, in addition to being a former Miss Illinois and spokesperson/activist for several charities. For more info about Heidi or for speaking or writing inquiries connect at HeidiRauld.com Heidi@HeidiRauld.com or facebook.com/heidirauld. For more info about the Rauld's companies visit SoleraVida.com and PremierLawGroup.net.

Life Changing Lesson of a Terrible Accident

By Kerstin Hardt

It was 15 years ago when I was on a skiing vacation in Arosa, one of the most beautiful winter resorts in the Swiss Alps. It was a wonderful day. The sun was shining. Anyone who has ever snowboarded knows the kind of feeling you experience gliding through the soft, powdered snow over frozen ground. I was floating down the slope with the wind in my face feeling pure bliss. Everything was perfect. Butterflies danced in my belly. I was completely happy. I felt invincible going faster, enjoying this feeling of absolute power and energy.

Then BANG!

Out of nowhere a skier crashed into me....

From that moment everything seemed to slide into slow motion; I felt my entire body lifting up. Then my head slammed down onto the ground. I felt the pressure of the hard impact on my whole body. I could not breathe. I became dizzy and everything was spinning. Every cell in my body was full of adrenaline; I was scared to death. I knew something was terribly wrong. My first thought was, "Dear God, please let me still be able to move!"

Before I realized, I was back in Germany in a hospital. They were scanning my body inch by inch in an MRI machine to see what had happened during the accident. I will never forget the banging noise of the magnets inside the tube. It was a fear inducing sound. After twenty long minutes, I was rolled out.

The doctor looked at me and asked, "What's your job, Kerstin?"

"I study sports and nutrition. I want to be a successful fitness, health, and life coach," I replied.

"You can forget that," he responded. "You have a badly slipped disc between the 5th and the 6th vertebrae. You will be able to move, but with this medical condition, you can forget your professional plans."

The orthopedic specialist I was referred to was chubby and non-athletic. He did not understand the life I was having to forget. He prescribed a neck brace, strong painkillers, and a six-month rehab plan. For my therapist, everything seemed clear. Business as usual. But, I was in shock. I had barely started my life. I thought to myself, was everything I had planned so carefully going to be of no value?

The next few days were hell on earth for me. I don't know how I survived, but I remember them as the worst days of my life. Do you know that feeling when all the avenues seem to close in front of you and everything looks bleak? I could see no way out. I felt terribly alone and so sorry for myself.

After a few days of utter misery and a lot of crying, my inner voice told me to stop complaining. Slowly my instincts for survival got the better of me and bit by bit I was able to shed my numbness. I started to wonder whether the doctor had to be right. Did he see the whole picture? He was only attending to my physical needs, but I wondered, what about the power of mind and soul that we supposedly possess? This was when I made an important decision.

I wasn't going to be defeated. I decided to be my own doctor and to take full responsibility for my body, my recovery, and my life. I wanted to be back in the driver's seat and be in charge. First, I got rid of that damned neck brace. I went to massages every day and started to do exercises that felt good to me. With my extensive knowledge of the human body, I devised an exact plan for my body to recover. The most important component I introduced was my mental training. I visualized a little man with an air pump blowing up my spinal disc. This visualization wasn't something I only performed once or twice. I did it over and over again, ten times a day or more. Day after day, I persevered.

After two weeks, I was pain free, and one week later I started my sports program at the university again. From this traumatic experience, I learned to take control and value the power of mind over matter.

Taking advice from the experts is one thing. Ultimately, it is up to you to be the judge of what is possible for your life. Advisors, friends, teachers, doctors, they all do the best they can, but they never have the full picture. Only you can know what you are capable of. You have an inner knowledge that you should listen to. As for the physical aspect, you can trust your body to take care of itself. It knows how your heart should beat, how your liver wants to detox, and how any ailment can be repaired. The key is to take control, listen to your intuition, and give your body and/or mind the permission to become active for you.

What happened to me was not a miracle. I made a conscious decision not to be defeated by circumstances. I put in every ounce of power and trust I could muster—and my body found the solution accordingly. Through my accident, I learned to take responsibility for how I think and act and present myself in life. I enjoyed a wonderful feeling of satisfaction when it worked the first time. Taking responsibility has become a habit since. As a matter of fact, it has become part of my personality now and it is a very gratifying experience.

Today I have achieved what I originally set out to do and more. I am happily married, running a successful sports and fitness coaching practice, sought after for advice by international companies and in demand as a speaker on the subject of life management. And all that is thanks to a life changing accident that required me to take responsibility and control. So, if you are in the face of a challenge take responsibility for your role in the situation. Whether it's mental training or physical action do everything that is necessary to stay in charge. You are the ultimate judge of what is good for you. In the end, it is your life.

TWEETABLE

Pay attention to your thoughts- they can come true. Mind over matter is the key to overcoming any circumstance.
—Kerstin Hardt #passionistas

Kerstin Hardt stands as one of the most successful health and life coaches in Germany, holding both lectures and seminars.

She studied sports and nutrition at the university in Mainz/Germany and did over 20 professional trainings in mental balance, yoga, meditation etc.

Read more about Kerstin on her web page: www.kerstin-hardt.com

Follow her on Facebook: www.facebook.com/KerstinHardt00
On Instagram: https://www.instagram.com/kerstin.hardt

Without a Fashion Background or Contacts, How Our Tote Bag Line Landed on the TODAY Show

By Cindy & Laura Massari

Have you ever had a great business idea that was nagging at you for years until finally you felt that you needed to take action or you would regret it for the rest of your life? That's how my mom, Cindy, felt the day our business was born. With no background experience in fashion or contacts in the industry, my mom and I pursued this dream and landed our product on the TODAY Show.

Our story proves that you can start anew by following your passions at any age and with hard work and a good partnership you can make waves with your business that you never thought possible.

It was October 2012; we were driving around in the car trying to find a pop-up shop to get ourselves Halloween costumes. I had been going through a funk in my personal life and felt lost. Cindy was hoping to cheer me up with this little outing and as fate would have it, we drove right past a fabric store. Even though fabric shopping was not on our itinerary for the day, Cindy immediately dodged into the parking lot. I didn't even bother to get out of the car. I had no interest in buying fabric or trying to start a new business in an industry neither of us had any experience in. My background is in finance, a far cry from fashion, and although Cindy has always loved fashion, she never had any experience in the field either.

Ten minutes later, Cindy came back with a bag full of various sparkly fabrics. With a look of focus and determination on her face she said, "I'm finally going to make this bag." It was going to be a new beginning for both of us. For ten years, my mom had talked passionately about wanting to make a chic fold up tote that she could carry to parties. She always found that she could never fit all her essentials in a clutch, and there was nothing else out there that was chic enough to carry when she was dressed up. Carrying a plastic or paper bag to a wedding was not an option, so she dreamed up the perfect tote bag to one day create.

Raising her children and dabbling in other interests along the way kept my mom from fulfilling this dream for many years. Although she talked about her idea with family and friends, she never knew where to begin. I watched this frustration grow with each day that passed. That evening on our mother-daughter venture, her dream had haunted her long enough. She believed it was now or never.

Initially, I was pretty disinterested and closed minded. I thought she was crazy for paying so much per yard of fabric and I couldn't imagine how she was going to make any money on it. But, that didn't stop her. At that time, she didn't care about making a profit. She just knew she was going to make a prototype and no one was going to stop her.

Soon after, she enlisted the help of a local seamstress to make the pattern. One day she excitedly came home with four bags and matching wristlets of each different colored fabric. Each one was beautiful and unlike anything I had ever seen before. I have to admit I was intrigued and impressed. She made a few more and started taking pictures with her cellphone and posting them on her personal Facebook page. Then, our first sale happened.

A friend of ours from California asked to buy a tote as a gift. I scrambled to figure out how we would accept payment since we didn't even have a website yet. I was so excited to close our first sale that I just had him pay us personally via PayPal. All it took was a moment of bravery and the guts to take a chance, and we had finally taken the first step down the path that Cindy had dreamed of for so long.

As the bags evolved those first few months, I became more involved. Cindy's passion for her newfound designs inspired me to jump in with full force. I learned how to set up a Limited Liability Corporation with the help of LegalZoom, participated in designing and selecting fabrics and researched as much as I could about setting up and running a website. At that point I felt that we were creating something amazing.

We called our company The Flip Flop Bitch™. The name came to be because Cindy loves to carry her flip flops with her in this bag to parties. People started to call her that and the name stuck. Together we believe a bitch is a woman who knows what she wants and isn't afraid to go get it! #ItsOkToBeABitch

For three years we continued to develop and market our totes. We attended tradeshows, sold online, emailed bloggers and TV networks, but we learned that it's not easy to get large scale exposure. Cindy kept saying she wanted to think bigger and outside of the box.

We had three big breaks. First was on the z100 radio show with Elvis Duran and Carla Marie, on which we were named the "what's trending" item.

Second was a feature on the Rachael Ray Show as a bridesmaid tote. Our biggest exposure was the day we were featured on the TODAY show.

One fateful day we had the opportunity to attend a free meet and greet with Kathie Lee Gifford at Bloomingdales. As big fans of Kathie and the show, it's safe to say we were ecstatic. Without any sales pitch, we gifted her one of our totes and said we hoped she would enjoy her very own Flip Flop Bitch™ tote.

Several weeks passed and we were sitting in our kitchen one morning with the TODAY Show playing in the background. Suddenly, the screen displayed a familiar sight. I squealed for mom to look at the screen. One of our bags was in Kathie Lee's hands being presented as one of her "Favorite Things" on the show! This moment continues to be a major highlight in our lives. As we watched Kathie Lee talk about our tote we hugged, cried, and jumped up and down with happiness. Finally, those early years of hard work had paid off!

We hadn't been notified in advance that our tote was going to be featured at all, let alone that morning. It was the most unexpected and wonderful surprise. If you ever read this, thank you so much Kathie Lee Gifford!

On our entrepreneurial journey, we learned that starting a new business will have many ups and downs. Here are some of the most important takeaways we want you to learn from our story:

1) You must be vigilant and protect your fledgling idea or business like a newborn baby. You will come across obstacles at every turn, including people who are not what they seem and who will take up your valuable time. People may reject you or your idea and make you feel like giving up. But, that's just it, the secret is to never give up on your passion. In the famous words of Gwen Stefani...#whatyouwaitingfor #takeachanceyoustupidwh**e

2) Find a business partner that compliments your skills, not replicates them. Diversity in thought process and skills is invaluable in business. I am more of a structured person and Cindy is definitely more creative and outgoing. I learned the importance of keeping an open mind and Cindy counts on me for running the logistics. Often, Cindy has come to me with some wild idea: a celebrity she wants to make a custom bag for or a cast of a TV show who should be using our bag. My job is to figure out how to get it done. I realized that without her wild ideas, we would have never had this business to begin with.

3) It's never too late and you're never too inexperienced to take the first step toward following your dream. Many women think that you need to be a

certain age to start a new business or that you need to have had a career or training in a given field. Cindy and I are thirty years apart and neither of us had any experience in fashion. Look at our adventures and how far we have come!

Keep going passionistas and one day we hope to see your business on the TODAY Show too!

Xoxo Cindy & Laura, The Flip Flop Bitches

TWEETABLE

Have you ever felt that you needed to take action in a certain moment or you would explode? #BitchesTakeAction #passionistas

Cindy and Laura Massari are a mother-daughter entrepreneurial team. Cindy is the CEO of The Flip Flop Bitch™. She has her M.A. in Education, is a trilingual, a Reiki Master, and a health & anti-aging beauty expert. Laura is a financial advisor, Certified Financial Planner®, partner in The Flip Flop Bitch™, and an artist/painter. Learn more at www.theflipflopbitch.com.

Moving Away from Pain and Towards Pleasure

By Kelli Calabrese

Early in life I found my passion, but it would take mental and physical work to overcome the obstacles I faced on my journey, as a passionista. When I was 13 years old, I wrote in my journal, "I will be an exercise therapist." At the time I had no idea what that meant, I just knew I wanted to move away from a very strong family history of heart disease, diabetes, obesity, alcoholism and cancer. I also realized I was happiest when I was dancing, swimming, playing softball, cheerleading or playing a game of tag in the yard.

I grew up in fear that my dad would never see me graduate high school, go to college, get married or have kids. At the age of 36 he was the oldest living male in his family. That fear of a sick life cut short and the love of fitness drove me to write this mission statement at the age of 17. "I will provide individuals with the tools to make health, fitness and wellness a permanent and enjoyable part of their lives." It has served me for decades!

I didn't focus on that pain and fear in this situation, rather I focused on moving closer to the positive, what I hoped to do. That determination prompted me to complete three science degrees by the age of 22, including a masters in clinical exercise physiology and cardiac rehabilitation. Before I graduated, I was a victim of a hit and run car accident and was broadsided in a high speed pursuit. Sidelined with subluxated discs, fractured ribs, a head injury and a dislocated knee, the doctors told me to choose a different profession than fitness. Again, I chose to move away from the pain (this time physical) and put my energy towards the pleasure of being rehabilitated and fulfilling my mission to help other people be healthy.

Over the course of the next decade I went on to own and operate a chain of health clubs, with over 200 employees, and manage corporate fitness centers for companies like Calvin Klein Cosmetics, BMW, Verizon and Beneficial Insurance. I co-founded a school that helped to prepare over 3,000 candidates to become certified fitness professionals and completed 25 certifications in fitness, wellness, nutrition & lifestyle coaching.

During this time my dad's health declined; however, I saw him give up alcohol, quit smoking, lose 60+ pounds and make healthier choices. Continuing to move towards the positive, I pushed further on my quest to reach more people. I became the lead fitness expert for eDiets, the largest subscription-based weight loss program at the time and also began doing media work to reach larger masses of people through TV, print, and digital media. Motivated to say yes to any opportunity that gave me a platform to help people walk in ultimate health, I became the fitness expert for Montel Williams and the editor of our industry's leading magazine for fitness pros. I even interviewed for Jillian Michael's position on the biggest loser, after being contacted by NBC.

Then a second car accident happened. A drunk driver fell asleep behind the wheel and hit me from behind. I sustained more damage to my neck and lower back, which once again fired me up to help more people be healthy. I knew that having strong muscles and being fit minimized my injuries and maximized my recovery. I was determined to set an example of perseverance and victory in the face of pain and adversity.

During this season, I became the international master trainer for Adventure Boot Camp and co-founded the IMPACT group fitness program. Together with my business partner, I was able to help hundreds of fitness professionals in nine countries fulfill their vision to become successful business owners and offer effective fitness programs. Six years ago I became an executive and top achiever with Isagenix International. This opportunity allowed me to provide nutrition solutions for over 10,000 people that not only lowers inflammation, acidity and toxicity, but also provides a proven and sustainable system for weight loss, energy, athletic performance and youthful aging. Coaching hundreds and even thousands of people motivated me more than ever to continue to provide effective, safe and proven fitness and nutrition solutions to a population whose health, due to obesity and disease, continues to decline.

What I have figured out is that, ultimately, life is going to hit you with things that are hard and painful and pose unexpected challenges. It's natural to want to move away from pain, yet some choose to dwell in pain and become immobilized by the emotions. Your choice to become a victim or a victor, however, is the differentiator in the outcome of your life. For me, I moved towards the pleasure of helping people wake up every morning being their physical best with no excuses. The pain can be used to fuel you to do something great. Your pain may be physical, financial, relational or professional. Consider how painful situations can give you leverage to not only be an overcomer yourself, but to help others overcome similar challenges.

My dad passed away at the age of 70 due to end stage heart, lung and kidney disease. He beat cancer three times and he pulled through double bypass surgery, kidney removal and living on dialysis. He was my inspiration—still is. He overcame the pain of addiction, obesity, cancer and many other hardships. He left a legacy on me and many others. His initial unhealthy choices in the early part of my life drove me to form good habits. Because of the choices to live in a healthy body and create wealth helping others, I was able to visit him 14 times in the last year of his life. While traveling from Dallas to New Jersey to visit him, I had the energy, health and lifestyle income to help my mom care for my dad in his final days.

If pain in life is inevitable, why not be prepared in every area of your life? As a wellness professional we use a wheel as a visual for each area of life including physical, spiritual, financial, relational, professional, personal, emotional, intellectual and environmental. The goal is to have each area balanced. While that is a moving target, I made a decision to do my very best daily to have every area of my life disciplined up as best as possible so that when situations arose, even despite my best efforts, they would not be a major issue for me. For example, if there was going to be another car accident, I would be in good physical health to recover faster, I would have the support of friends and family to help with any daily needs, I would have access to the best doctors and therapists, money would be abundant if I had needs that exceeded insurance, I would have residual income regardless of if I am able to work and I can always trust in God!

Spend your days moving towards what gives you pleasure so that when that phone call comes, that less than excellent news is delivered, or plans somehow fall short, you have excellence in other areas of your life so you can quickly recover and grow in your areas of passion.

I challenge you to look at the past and present pain in your life. Look at what brings you pleasure, your passions. Consider how you can use the pain as a catalyst, using any energy you have to focus and move towards your happiness. As you do this, doors of opportunity will open and it will be up to you to decide to create change from your pain and with your passions. This is the road to finding your purpose. Take it!

TWEETABLE
Move away from pain & towards passion to set you on the path towards purpose #MoveTowardsYourPurpose #FromPaintoPurpose #FromPaintoPassion

Kelli Calabrese is a 30+ year fitness, nutrition, & lifestyle expert leading people to be their best spirit, mind & body. Through her speaking, books & solutions, she'll inspire you to enjoy a fit, energized body, financial freedom and a joy-filled life. Kelli is an executive and top achiever with Isagenix International and a co-author of Mom and Dadpreneur. She is wife of 23 years to Anthony and mom to two amazing teens Nicholas and Melina. www.KelliCalabrese.com 469-744-9154.

Kelli@KelliCalabrese.com

www.Facebook.com/KelliCalabrese

Out Writer:
A Story of Sexuality
and Courage

By Takara Sights

I wouldn't have the courage to chase my dream of being a successful writer today if I hadn't come out first. That's because deciding to be honest about my deepest passions was a lot like telling people about my sexuality. After years of hiding, telling people who I was inside helped me not only accept, but also love myself. Changing the way I presented myself to the world was the most difficult and rewarding thing I've ever done. I am now the happiest I have ever been because I have found the courage to live authentically.

Long before I came out, I wouldn't even admit to myself that I was attracted to women as well as men. I started having feelings around the same time all children do. When I came to understand those feelings, I denied them. I buried them, ignored them, and reasoned them away.

Using energy to lie and hide my genuine feelings was painful. It damaged my relationships because I felt that no one knew me. I was alone and depressed. I didn't think I could ever feel differently so I didn't want to try. I wanted to quit. I thought about how much easier it would be if I killed myself. Sometimes it seemed like the right thing to do.

When you keep something inside, this kind of suffering is inevitable. Hiding part of yourself is poisonous, whether it is queerness or a dream. Everyone needs time to discover and accept who they are. Some people, like me, take longer because they are afraid of what people will think of them. When I let everyone see the real me, I would be making myself vulnerable. I didn't think I could handle it.

I accepted that I was attracted to women in the middle of the night, alone, in my loft bed at University of San Francisco. I was relieved to know the truth. Lying was using so much energy. Energy I could have been using to grow.

I struggled with the knowledge at first. I woke up at seven every day to run for an hour on the treadmill while reading about the feats of Charles Darwin. I talked to Counseling and Psychological Services about everything that didn't have to do with what I was dealing with. I drank. I ignored my understanding and hid it from the world.

Three years later, when I was strong enough to come out to my friends in the middle of the night at Trader Sam's tiki bar, I was relieved. I finally reclaimed the energy I had been using to hide from them.

I came out to my family next, slowly, one person at a time. I told them in the middle of the night in a pitch-black basement bedroom in Maui, on a sunny day at a Giant's game, in my office over the phone, and once by text message.

Telling my mom was the most difficult. It was the most painful conversation I've ever had. When I told her the truth, I died in her mind. She told me she could understand why parents of gay children kick them out of the house. She saw me as a stranger. I was blindsided.

Those feelings are hard to forget, but I did heal. I feel we are closer now than ever because I'm not wearing a mask and shield. Today, my mom is my biggest mentor and support system. I would not be anywhere near where I am today without her emotional, spiritual, and major financial support.

I think coming out stories like mine are powerful because, in a way, they are universal. We all struggle with aspects of who we are. Straight people. White people. Rich people too.

I found that being honest about my sexuality helped me discover the courage to accept the rest of me. If I could be honest about who I am attracted to, I felt that I could share anything. If it was possible for me to exist as a queer, black, American woman, who is happy, I could be anything. It didn't happen all at once. This process took years, but it began when I realized the pain I was in was more terrible than the possibility of rejection.

Although my personal life was maturing, my professional life was stunted. I felt like I was not in control. Going to work gave me stomach aches, rashes, and a feeling of dread. Fortunately, the universe showed me another way.

After I began studying business, I told myself that I would be an entrepreneur one day. That "one day" was a way of holding myself back, a way of protecting myself from the failure and judgment I thought I would face as an entrepreneur. Before I could start my own business, I thought I would have to be older, have more money, be more experienced, and know more people. But, those thoughts were really excuses, just like the excuses I used to keep myself safe in the closet.

Entrepreneurship is popular today. Steve Jobs and Elon Musk make it sexy. But, to be an entrepreneur is still to be "other." Others make people uncomfortable. I was afraid that people would judge me for being an entrepreneur, just as I was afraid to come out about my sexuality.

This changed, midday, in a buffet line. I heard myself say, "I am an entrepreneur." Then, the switch flipped. I realized the uncertainty I felt about my future was greater than my fear of failure and judgment, so I took action. From there, it felt easy to start my first business, Earth & Sky Works.

Like so many first businesses, Earth & Sky Works was a stepping stone. I launched it to teach me about the vast world of sales and online marketing. At that, it was successful! It grew to be a private-label Amazon business focused on eco-friendly products and a design & DIY blog. To expand fast so I could pay the bills I read books, listened to podcasts, and attended every seminar, summit, and mastermind I could. At one of these events, I made the connection that led me to my work today, work that I am in love with.

After attending Brian Tracy's 2016 Success Mastery Academy, I rediscovered my love for writing. After going through the process of coming out and thriving, it has become much easier to accept and share new identities as I continue to develop. When I remembered I was a writer I was ready to share my skillset with anyone who cared to ask. When Marketer and *Passionistas* Publisher Kyle Wilson announced on Facebook that he was looking for an editor and project manager for his next few books, I raised my hand, even though I was sure I was under qualified. Whether or not that's true, I am thrilled he said yes and I get to be part of the *Passionistas* team and get paid for it! I am dancing at the thought of using my writing, editing, and organization skills to help others tell their stories in future Lessons From Network books.

You can gain the same courage if you lean into your fear. If you're in pain and hiding part of who you are, remember, it's more painful to try to be the person you think other people want you to be than it is to be yourself. I hope my story shows you what you might have. When your outside and inside are in harmony you will feel whole. Be honest with yourself. Love yourself. Then, welcome others to see who you are.

TWEETABLE

It's more painful to be the person you think other people want you to be than it is to just be yourself #lifeworthliving #courage

Takara Sights is a writer, editor, entrepreneur, and animal enthusiast. She is proud Passionistas Editor and Project Manager. Above all else, Takara loves her dog, hearing great stories, and sharing amazing food. Stay tuned for wicked collaborations between sisters Takara and writer, actress and comedian Reed Sights.

Connect at www.takarasights.com

Facebook: Takara Sights | Instagram: takara_sights

The "Never Give Up"

By Tabitha Lipkin

I remember the first time I heard it...

I was on the red carpet of SXSW in 2010 interviewing Jodie Foster for the University of Texas and I asked for advice on behalf of those going into the media industry. "Never give up" was the answer and, to this day, the people I know who are the most successful in their fields follow that advice to a tee.

It seems like obvious advice, "never give up," but it's the kind of advice that doesn't come with too much lace. Meaning, it is the key to success, if you know how to interpret it. "Never give up" doesn't include instructions on how to turn the key and when to open the door. It only includes what may seem like something you'd read on the side of a Wheaties box.

I don't have any specific moments in my life that led to one grand "ahhhh" moment. I've had and continue to have experiences with little "ahhhh" moments when I feel like I complete or take on a new challenge. People who know me think that I've accomplished so much, but, in reality, I'm never satisfied. And, in turn, I "never give up" on finding those little "ahhhhh" moments in my career because with each one I move closer to the big "ahhhhh" moment I've always dreamed of.

I want to break down what it means to not give up. It's not as simple as settling. OH NO! It's much more complex than that. There will be times in your career, regardless of your profession, when things are not going to work out. You must persevere through those moments. It's certainly not as easy as it sounds, but nothing worth fighting for is ever easy.

There have been times in my life when I had less then $10 in my bank account and not a single person or place to fall back on. There have been times when nothing, literally nothing, was going right, not in my professional life or home life. There have been times when I was the only person who believed I could do something. And, there have been times when I didn't want to keep going. What helped me get to where I am today, as someone who does everything from report the news, to travel the world, to literally anything I want to do, is remembering those three words... "Never Give Up."

If I gave up during times that I wanted to, I honestly might be stuck bartending... or possibly working behind the scenes in production. Those were not my dreams. I knew that "If it was easy... everyone would do it..." So I took the knowledge that what I was doing was hard, and I accepted that it was hard for a good reason.

The truth is, the ones who are successful in any industry are not necessarily the best at their jobs or most qualified. They are the ones who didn't give up. Now, imagine that you have the opportunity to be the most qualified and the best at your job and you refuse to give up… that is what will make you a grand success.

Going back to those little "ahhhhh" moments, part of the "never give up" mindset is also not falling into or settling for those small "ahhhhh" moments. Those moments are certainly meant to be enjoyed and will help you on your journey, but take into account how exactly those moments will help you grow. Do it with class, do it with kindness, and do it in a way that others can't help but notice you. But, above all else, do YOU.

With a persistent mindset, you can do anything you set your mind to. Set your mind toward your goals and be the person you want to be. "Never Give Up," that's the key to being a leader and being the ultimate #GirlBoss.

TWEETABLE
@tabithalipkin 'It seems like obvious advice, "never give up," but it's the kind of advice that doesn't come with too much lace' #girlboss

Tabitha Lipkin is a TV Personality, Comedian, Dive Master, Sailor, World Traveler, Former Miss Scuba International, and all around Water Bug.

You can connect at: www.tabithalipkin.com

@TabithaLipkinOfficial on Facebook

@TabithaLipkin on Instagram/Twitter

Beauty in Depth: A Journey of Personal Transformation

By Christina Rendon

Learning transformational tools and holistic lifestyle practices allowed me to transform my life beyond what I could have ever imagined. Through diving deep into self-work, I began a journey that built me up and supported my well-being. The process of learning to heal myself began with an awakening.

With a new level of awareness I began a journey of improving my health, emotions, mental state, and spirituality. Meditation and working with spiritual teachers also allowed me to access a greater peace and deep wisdom of life. Throughout my healing process, I learned the importance of self-work in achieving success and fulfillment in all levels of life.

As a young woman in 2007, I was at a place where self-reflection caused me to realize I could not continue the lifestyle I was living and feel fulfilled or truly thrive. I indulged in destructive behaviors, patterns, and coping mechanisms including addictions and an unhealthy lifestyle, which were keeping me from facing the underlying pain in my life.

These patterns were greatly affecting my health, my happiness, and my ability to connect with others. Also, I was limiting myself by not being grateful for my life, my body, and the qualities I had. I realized the pain I felt was only an opportunity for me to evaluate why I was not loving myself and to go deeper within my being to heal. I wanted to experience more bliss and connection with people and to express more of my potential. Most importantly, I realized that it was essential for me to develop more self-love.

My healing began with self-examination and a decision to truly be happy as well as the desire to complete the cycle by uplifting others. I transformed my life into a healthier pathway and moved towards my potential by improving the way I treated and talked to myself and choosing to empower myself. This path led me to reconnect to my intuition and spirituality, as well as improve my nutrition. I felt a great shift. A deep peace pervaded my life. Through this connection, I felt a sense of power, clarity, and miraculous release from old patterns that were holding me back.

Journaling helped me to make practical shifts in my life. One day I felt inspired to create a list of what would truly make me happy and what was holding me back from being happy. I then began acting on the goals that I wished to achieve and resolving the things that I was holding onto. I started eating healthier, started giving more, started sharing with people how I was really feeling, and started to express my creativity.

Part of my happiness came from being able to accept myself and express my truth. The transformation I experienced allowed me to develop an empathy and compassion for people and myself. I awakened spiritually and creatively to the feeling that I was here to inspire and share light with everyone I connected with. My priorities shifted and the only things that I wanted to focus on were connecting spiritually, building myself up, living a healthy lifestyle, and being loving. Self-discovery and making real lifestyle shifts that supported my healing and self-expression allowed me to achieve new potentials in my life.

During the summer of 2008, prior to my enrollment in college, a family friend recommended an intrapersonal communications course with an amazing teacher. I'll never forget the first day of that spring semester, when I walked in to meet that professor; she had an aura of magic, openness and compassion. I was already on a journey of self-study and was following my intuition of what I thought was best for my healing. However, this class gave me an opportunity to learn many transformational tools that I had not yet been exposed to.

I spent the next 16 weeks immersed in fascinating teachings about brain frequencies and rewiring, alchemy, quantum physics, meditation, intuition, and alternative health. Most importantly, this class accelerated my exploration of my own consciousness and assisted my intrapersonal relationship. I began implementing more of what I was learning to shift my life and began to experience more positivity and inspiration.

At the end of the semester when I thanked the professor, she responded, "When the student is ready the teacher appears." Along my journey of self-work I continued to have similar synchronicity with the people I met and experiences I had.

In 2009, I enrolled in a spiritual and personal transformational school, where I learned energy healings and many techniques that I felt empowered by. I deepened my understanding of meditation and learned techniques that allowed me to feel an immense flow of light in my life. Through my studies with my teachers I worked on cultivating a deep presence and really getting in touch with my heart. One of my teachers would constantly remind us that everything is an opportunity to choose either love or fear. All of the changes I made from 2007 to that point transformed my reality and I was actively shifting my emotions, energy, and life.

Then, after three years on my journey of self-work, I slipped into self-defeating habits around health and my ability to stay positive. I was unsure of who to turn to. I doubted that there were many people who could relate to where I was and how to truly help me evolve to a higher place. This led me to find new mentors who were experts in creating core transformation.

I spent one year rediscovering myself, my life, and my being. The life I wanted required me to go deeper. The challenge was actually an 'opportunity for growth' and my body whispering for me to look at things that I hadn't fully dealt with. When we are out of alignment, we'll sometimes get a whisper to redirect that will continue to intensify to a scream until we listen.

> *When we are out of alignment, we'll sometimes get a whisper to redirect that will continue to intensify to a scream until we listen.*

Through this new level of healing, I learned to deeply forgive and create true connection with myself and others. Instead of just allowing myself to be what I perceived as light, I chose to accept all aspects of myself. I learned to accept the array of my being and feel, deal, and heal. The contrast in the increase in self-love and self-care from how I once I felt made me passionate and dedicated to living in a way that builds me up. Happiness and healing became accessible through choosing to have compassion, living in gratitude, practicing meditation, and living a healthy lifestyle.

> *Happiness and healing became accessible through choosing to have compassion, living in gratitude, practicing meditation, and living a healthy lifestyle.*

After years of learning about myself and working with experts in personal transformation, I began implementing the practices in my life on a new level. I transferred from community college into UCLA in 2012 by using many of the methods I learned about manifesting and achieving goals. I practiced visualization, gratitude, maintaining my energy and health, and communicating in an authentic way. Outside of school, I continued with health mentors and spiritual teachers.

In 2012, I incorporated a living foods, plant-based lifestyle. I had already been plant-based for four years prior, although I noticed that the more living plant-based foods I ate, the better I felt. My skin got better than ever before and my mood and body seemed to balance out more than ever before. My overall life transformed through knowing myself, actively shifting patterns I had, and being healthier. This became possible because of the leap I took into looking into how I was treating my body, mind, and soul and how that was impacting my life.

I spent the next years captivated and enchanted by the body's ability to heal emotionally through perspective shift and physically through holistic practices. True healing comes from realizing the interconnectedness of mind, body, and spirit and coming into harmony with one's being and the environment. The experiences I've had have helped me realize the power in choosing my emotional state and changing my story's meaning.

> *True healing comes from realizing the interconnectedness of mind, body, and spirit and coming into harmony with one's being and the environment.*

For me, everything seemed to flow effortlessly after committing to self-work. I have learned from, interviewed, and taken courses with some of the world's leading health educators, spiritual teachers, and entrepreneurs. Now, when I lead group meditations and gatherings, create and share inspirational content, or work with people in collaborative settings, I feel grateful to have a place inside where I can be authentic and creative. I was able to go from destructive habits to living a life full of love and inspiration by transforming from within.

Self-work is a consistent practice that allows us to achieve more in all areas in our life. We are able to have clarity on what we truly desire and a deeper connection with life through self-awareness. There are many practices that allow for self-awareness. The key is to find the ones that help you become your greatest self. Whether it be through taking a course, journaling, or meditating, self-reflection is a great tool for growth. Begin journaling to see how you feel, how you want to feel and how you can get there. We all have gifts to give to the world and when we're in alignment with ourselves the universe supports us.

TWEETABLE
Follow your inspiration, live your truth, and fulfill your authentic, greatest potential.
— Christina Rendon #passionistas

Christina Rendon is a certified holistic lifestyle coach and wellness consultant. Christina provides clients content marketing strategies and offers mindfulness and wellness training services that enhance productivity and wellbeing. Christina's passion is to inspire and motivate individuals to achieve their greatest personal and professional potential in life. She achieves this through meditation guidance, energy healing, and living-food education. Connect with her at: ChristinaRendon.com, Christina.M.Rendon@gmail.com

Helping Others Create Freedom and Legacy

By Kimberly Schmidtke

If you believe in yourself, anything is possible. I'm a mother of three boys: Calvin, 27, Barrett, 25, and Tucker, 24. They have always been my why. I have worked so hard to build a global business where I earn more in a month than I did in a year at my corporate job because I want to build a legacy for my sons. When I started relationship marketing several years ago I discovered another why: impacting lives all over the world.

When I first got into relationship marketing, I experienced building in a couple different companies. I absolutely loved it and I met so many wonderful friends, but I wasn't successful at all. There was no simple system for me to plug into. When there isn't a simple system a lot of times confusion sets in and momentum is not created. That's what happened for me. I believe if you want to massively duplicate a business it has got to be from the word simplicity. So often potential entrepreneurs look at a business and think "Is it too good to be true?" or "Can I do it and will somebody help me?"

I always say: fancy doesn't duplicate!

Almost five years ago I was introduced to the company I'm with now. I absolutely love and am so grateful to my dear friend who introduced it to me. At the time, I was not interested whatsoever. I really didn't think that this industry was cut out for me, especially because of my previous lack of success. But, I wanted to listen to my friend because I could tell she was super excited about what she was doing.

She told me that there had been an accidental discovery at a cancer research hospital that I was really familiar with. As it turned out, my father, who was so near and dear to me, had reached out to THAT hospital when he had pancreatic cancer. It felt like a sign. I wondered, "What if this is the company?" I imagined building a legacy for my family and impacting lives all over the world. So, I decided to just take a leap of faith and I've never ever looked back.

I started right in the beginning with an absolutely burning desire to win for my team and to help as many people as possible in the business win. From when I was a little girl I had parents who really believed in me. One of my biggest gifts is that I've been able to carry that over and believe in others. I believe they are champions that they are destined for greatness, that they have been put on this Earth to impact lives. Everyone is destined for greatness; everyone has a purpose, but it all comes from within. You can't give people the burning desire necessary to succeed. They've got to have it. You can give them tools and training, but you can't give them desire. It comes with making the decision. You can't just dream about it. You can't just think about it. You have to go out and decide that you are going to make a difference and that you are going to impact lives. I had my burning desire because I wanted to make a difference in the world.

With this mindset I began building a team. It truly was little win after little win strung together to create the success we have today. Our team now has reached over 20,000 brand partners in five countries. We have many other countries that are going to open up soon. The company, Nerium, is now a billion dollar company and it's on track to be a multi-billion dollar company.

I am so grateful for the opportunity to be a part of something that is having such a big impact on the lives of others. I've definitely experienced setbacks in this business and difficult times, but I always stay consistent and I've always taken perseverance to the highest level you can ever imagine. It's not an overnight deal; success doesn't just appear. I just know in my heart that the sky's the limit, especially when you can build a business that you love and that you are passionate about. I'm passionate about helping other people experience the freedom I have. With my freedom I am living my ultimate life: providing for my family and supporting my favorite charities while traveling with my friends and spending time with my sons.

I am sharing my story because I want to instill the confidence in others to achieve greatness in life. When you climb these mountains with purpose, focus on helping others win, get yourself out of the way, and do it with love and happiness you can conquer any obstacle you can imagine. In whatever you do, try to add value to your relationships. What you add will come back to you. Living your life in a way that benefits other people will be your pathway to success.

TWEETABLE
Fancy doesn't duplicate. Simplicity works.
—Kimberly Schmidtke #passionistas #keepitsimple #nerium

Kimberly Schmidtke built her business in breakthrough anti-aging products at Nerium by believing in others. Kimberly is thrilled to be featured twice in Success Magazine and to be earning more in one month than she earned in one year at her corporate job, but the real benefit is the freedom to spend time with her three adult sons, Calvin, Barrett, and Tucker.

Learn more: kaglobal.nerium.com

Contact: (253)514-9847.

Clearly Heal Any Fear

By Melissa Laine

f you believe in yourself, anything is possible." at the beginning of her story. On many occasions fear is a roadblock on our path toward a specific goal or action. The best way to get through fear is to recognize it and push through it. Even when your ego creates various excuses as to why you shouldn't, allow yourself to feel the fear. Let the emotions power your ability to knock it down and achieve your desires.

I know this method works because I have used it to establish myself as a coach who helps others move past their fears to create their dreams. Though it is difficult, there is power in recognizing our fears. For, in this conscious state, we can make the choice to move forward.

Confidently establishing my worth was, for many years, a fear of mine. I remember when a bride to be, who was one of the first clients for the wedding videography business I started in high school, told me I was ambitious.

The bride to be and her fiancé sat in my parents' home one afternoon, in the room I once used for crafting and playing. I had transformed it into my very own office to showcase samples of my work to potential clients and explain my services (this was before the Internet was able to handle shared user generated video content and long before YouTube).

As a high school student, discussing payment for my services always made me nervous. I thought, who would pay me to film one of the most precious events of their life? I was fearful of establishing my worth by charging too much, or too little. I knew I had to present my value in reflection to my talents, yet I wanted to get the sale without undercutting myself. I thought, am I worthy of charging this price? Do I have the credibility or experience?

Some of these questions of doubt still come up for me today when starting a new service or playing with new business ideas. It's a fear many entrepreneurs struggle with.

I knew that despite my fears I had to go through with it. After telling her my price and finalizing the contract, she asked me how old I was. "I'm 16," I said.

"Well, you're ambitious," she responded.

All I could think was "Well, of course." I didn't really know or feel that what I was doing was ambitious. There was no fear, no doubt in my mind that

I should be a wedding videographer at a young age. It was only when I thought of what others would think or when I questioned their belief in me, that I would doubt myself. Most high school students don't run their own business and employ their mom. Because my situation was out of the norm, I had fear. But, I didn't let this fear hold me back because it would not have brought me customers or money.

Despite my ambitious spirit, I grew up shy. I was comfortable having a few close friends yet felt out of place in larger groups. I wasn't very popular due to my shyness of connecting with others on deeper levels and fear of not being accepted for who I really was.

I had an experience where boys in grade school made fun of me for being too tall. They called me ogre because I was taller than the rest of my friends. My young impressionable self interpreted this as a story of boys thinking that I wasn't pretty, which led me to feel unlovable. These emotions came forward the day I decided to do something I wanted to do for a while, beauty pageants. The best thing I learned through doing pageants, however, is that you are really competing against yourself and your own insecurities. Entering in a beauty pageant was a healing experience because, even though I felt those insecurities, I recognized them and moved forward anyway.

Going through these experiences at a young age was not easy. But, what I've learned is to feel your fear and do it anyway.

Even though I grew up learning this method and used it, later in my life I found it hard to act on it.

I found myself living with a boyfriend who, unbeknownst to me, had an addiction issue. By the time I found out, it was too late and I had to move out. It took me a while to decide to breakup and move because I thought I finally had it all together. I was with the guy I loved. We shared a nice house together and it was comfortable. I didn't want to leave that for the unknown of no job, no money, and no place to live. Yet, the alternative of living with an addict was not an option for me. I faced my fear of not knowing how I was going to support myself and packed up my things in one day, not knowing where I was going to stay that night. I vowed to myself to create a coaching business that would help other women build their passion businesses so they would never have to be in a place where they would have to go through what I went through.

As I moved into adulthood, I stopped trying to win acceptance from other people. I stopped trying to be popular by conforming to others' standards and I stopped really caring what others thought of me. So much so that I gained the confidence to try stand up comedy. I believe it's a true test to see if you care what others think of you. With stand up comedy you share your deep dark stories and try to make light of them in a joke.

It became a healing experience for me as I used stand up comedy as therapy to overcome that bad break up. At my first open mic I was scared, especially after hearing "you better be good" from a stranger. I didn't let the fear get the best of me. Later that night I was offered to be introduced to the owners of a famous comedy club. On my second open mic I was scouted to perform in an all female comedy show. My third time performing was at the all female show.

Had I been intimated and let the fear get the best of me, I wouldn't have known how far I could go so quickly.

I realized that self-doubt was a negative pattern in my life. We all have negative patterns we've picked up from childhood, from our parents, and our upbringing. When we practice inner healing and we decide to become aware, we create more space for us to confidently show up in the world. Awareness is consciousness. Recognizing a block such as fear or self-doubt is an accomplishment because it shows that you are taking a step closer to overcoming your obstacles and thus moving you forward to reach your goal. We can go to as many self-empowerment workshops as we want, but as long as we can recognize our limiting patterns and move forward, healing can take place.

After my pageant days, I went on to offer my own coaching service, going from contestant to coach, helping girls in the process of developing their inner beauty in preparation for beauty pageants. Today, I am The Clearing Coach, helping clients remove blocks and obstacles towards achieving their dreams through working on clearing their energy around negative thought patterns and beliefs. I'm offering the coaching I wish I had received when I needed it the most.

I've been on a healing/ healer's path since I graduated from college. There is always something to be healed. There is always something we can work on to improve ourselves. The quickest and easiest way on any healing path is to simply feel your fear and move forward toward your goal anyway, no matter what!

TWEETABLE

Clear any fear by feeling it and then moving forward, towards the action of that fear. Do something that scares you for it will free you!

Melissa Laine, The Clearing Coach, helps multi-passionate millennials get clear while removing blocks towards creating their business. She is the creator of "Find Your Passion & Profit," a 3 step process that sets up her clients for success in 3 months!

Melissa is a trained Reiki Master, Emotional Freedom Technique EFT/ Tapping Practitioner, Sound Healer and Intuitive Reader. TheClearingCoach.com

Instagram: the_clearing_coach

Twitter: melissalaine.

Facebook: ClearingCoachMelissaLaine

Your Biggest Breakthrough is Born at Rock Bottom

By Jessica Joy Reveles

The room is large and tidy and bright. There are two low children's bookshelves in one corner, a bin brimming with Barbies and toy trucks, a blue patterned rug, and a round white table with a pitcher of water and tiny paper cups on a plastic lunch tray. And bunkbeds, twelve of them lined up against the walls. In all we are nearly thirty single mothers and children hailing from different parts of Los Angeles. We have one undeniable thing in common. We are homeless.

It's the second time I have been homeless in eight years. This isn't the story I imagined I'd tell when sitting down to write about success. But it's the truth. And strangely, as undesirable as my current circumstances might appear from the outside looking in, I'm not angry or even embarrassed. Instead, I'm grateful. Because at thirty-two I know something for certain: there is a breakthrough on the horizon if only I keep my gaze there.

This is Our New Normal

But it's a slippery slope. I live with bipolar I, obsessive compulsive disorder, anxiety, and chronic pain. Success, for me, has taken many shapes over the years. Sometimes it's flashy and festive like giving a keynote or receiving an award. Other times it's meager: getting dressed, locking the door two times instead of twenty, ignoring the pain in my body. I talk myself through each day, plot my steps as though navigating points on a map. I'm bad with maps. I confess, I don't have a five-year plan. Hell, I don't even have a six-month plan. Which doesn't mean I don't have goals. I've just learned that the best way for me to manage my illness and my life is literally one day at a time.

At the local family shelter where my son and I currently reside, one day at a time is a full schedule and there's no time to feel sorry for myself or sink into all too familiar depression. I'm up at 5 a.m., eating breakfast with my son by 6:30 a.m., and out the door to drop him off at school at 7:15 a.m. I hustle all day, working multiple jobs and as many hours as possible. The shelter reopens for dinner at 6 p.m. Then there are chores, tutoring for the kids, and class or counseling for the parents. Bath and bedtime follow, and lights are out at 9 p.m.

The room goes dark, but not quiet. Many of the kids are around my son's age—six, seven, eight. Some of them whimper and whine, others cry out loudly, a few do fall asleep right away. I close my eyes tight, a futile attempt to sleep. My body aches with so much tension, holding the weight of weeks spent packing and moving boxes into storage and furniture into friends' garages. There aren't any tears left to cry. And really, I'm more relieved than anything else. This is our new normal.

My eyes flutter open as suddenly the top bunk shifts. I hear tiny feet coming down the ladder. My son crawls into bed next to me; rests his chin on my shoulder; and whispers, I love you, wrapping his arms and legs around my tired body. For just a moment I'm transported. We're in our own home again, it's just the two of us and our black-and-white cat, and it's quiet. I slip into a light sleep, waking every hour until dawn. One day at a time.

I Started Saying Yes

Rather than succumb to overwhelm and exhaustion, I embrace every aspect of my situation—the good, the bad, and the very ugly. Even though there isn't enough money to pay my bills or keep my bank account in the black. Even though my credit has tanked. Even though I don't know when or how I'll ever get ahead. I have hope. Because it's when we're at our lowest that the most primal trait we have within us sparks—the will to survive. And in my experience, survival also has the potential to promote ingenuity and breed success. Everything counts. Today I measure success not in terms of how many notches I can add to my resume, but by the small wins—which are actually a big deal. I looked in the mirror and smiled at the woman looking back. I made my son laugh. I comforted a friend. I let a friend comfort me.

I've come a long way since I was pregnant and homeless at twenty-four. Then I was resentful, lost, and severely struggling with my mental illness. It was a long road to stability, and I worked hard to keep my life together once I got back on my feet. When I turned thirty I still had problems, but something shifted. I stopped being so angry. I eliminated negativity from my life including toxic relationships with family, friends, and lovers. And I became fearless in the pursuit of my passions.

I started saying yes. Yes to opportunity. Yes to volunteering in my community. Yes to healthy relationships, and most importantly, yes to myself. I finally found peace and self-acceptance. And everything changed. I became genuinely happy and that happiness radiated across every area of my life. I worked up the courage to leave my corporate job and committed to building my business, a boutique marketing and social media firm. It's been more than a bumpy road, but I believe I landed here—homeless—for a reason. And I believe that rock bottom is where the biggest breakthroughs are born. Now there is only one option: make it work.

Maybe the goal isn't to succeed in the traditional sense. Because in reality, success is so subjective. It looks and feels different for everyone. On my most successful days I show up, put one foot in front of the other, and find as many reasons as possible to be grateful. Each passing day it becomes easier to do this, and I move a step in the right direction. Unbelievably, I can even say I am grateful to be homeless. And I really am. Because it's being in this situation that's forced me to fight for my life, fight for my son, and fight for my business. It's getting out of this situation that will make the rewards more meaningful. Success is seeing possibility when everything feels like it's falling apart.

I don't believe we can ever be prepared for the moments that change our lives. I know I've never been. But I've learned to savor each one because from one moment to the next, our lives have the potential to take unexpected turns.

Every moment is so precious. And homeless or not, I think that's what we're all striving for—to drink in the moments that make up our lives. If we can do that with gratitude and let everything else melt away, I would call that success. I would call that a breakthrough.

TWEETABLE

#success is so subjective. It looks and feels different for everyone, and it's all about #smallwins #redefinesuccess #liveinthemoment

Jessica Joy Reveles is a seasoned writer and editor with nearly 15 years of integrated marketing including social media, advertising, digital publishing, instructional design, and teaching experience across health & wellness, fashion & beauty, and lifestyle. Solution oriented and meticulous, she brings a solid foundation in digital communications with an emphasis on research, strategy, branding, analytics, and more.

www.jessicajoyreveles.com | hello@jessicajoyreveles.com

How Networking Smart Led Me Into Hollywood

By Andria Schultz

"How did you get into the film industry and network smart?" seems to be one of the many questions I frequently get asked. I began to learn how when I landed my first job in Hollywood. There is no guaranteed handbook on networking in the film industry, however, I can give you tips on how to network the smart way.

After working for TV shows like: Your Family Matters, America's Funniest Home Videos, The Real Daytime, Disney Channel's: Bizaardvark, NCIS, and more, I learned that networking takes hard work and patience. It was challenging to get to where I am today, and I still struggle on the path to further success. Despite the negativity and mishaps, I haven't given up. It's important when you are trying to find your networking skills to focus on being positive and true to yourself.

Since the age of eight, I knew I wanted to be part of the film industry. My goal was to become the next CEO of Disney, but the question was how would I get there? I knew I needed experience for anyone to take me seriously, so I began dabbling with my father's camcorder and convinced all of my childhood friends to be part of my homemade movies.

Naturally, I was a determined child. I wasn't afraid to approach and ask people the necessary questions to better myself. My parents always insisted that I shouldn't be afraid of dreaming and setting high standards for myself. My mother insisted that I take classes to enhance my self-esteem and, through those classes in dancing, speech, cooking, sports, and more, I learned how to be a well-rounded individual. With my parents' continuous support I was able to become the confident young networker I am today.

Learning how to network means that you ultimately need to find someone who you can trust and share your passion with. Having and serving as a mentor are the best ways to create your network foundation. I believe there are three different types of mentors in your life: physical, mental, and spiritual. It doesn't matter how many you have in each category so long as you have each of them.

Do not be afraid to ask someone to be your mentor, always be yourself, and find passion in talking with people. The outreach must derive from your heart.

Early into my teenage years, I began my journey by seeking a mentor. I approached Constance Ramos from Extreme Makeover Home Edition, while at church one Sunday. Inexperienced and without full understanding of what I would be enduring, I greeted her with confidence. She looked at me and smiled saying, "Honey, you are so young, come back to me when you are serious about the film industry."

As a young passionista, I went back to her a few years later telling her that I was ready. She recommended we meet for lunch and that was when everything changed for me. Indirectly, I was paving my path to becoming a passionista. When you aren't afraid of expressing yourself, the universe works on making your dreams into reality.

Constance gave me the confidence I needed to move forward as a woman in an industry ruled by men. She advised me to build "elephant skin" or tough skin. She sat with me for hours telling me her stories and advice. As I went on to build my network I found that my self-confidence grew, my network became stronger.

My network grew at an incremental pace and it allowed me to mingle with people I never thought possible. At sixteen, I got my first internship with a company named Manorge Productions where I was able to put to practice everything that Constance had taught me.

I initially got this internship because I went through a newspaper and saw that they were looking for an intern with Photoshop experience. Without knowing anything about Photoshop, I still took the initiative to reach out to the CEO of the company and landed a one-on-one interview. During this interview, I showed everything that I was capable of doing: drawing, marketing, people skills, etc. I did whatever it took to captivate his interest. I made sure to mention I would take a Photoshop class at the community college if need be. That comment alone landed me the position and I kept my word.

A few years later, the opportunity to be an Executive Producer for a television and radio show arose. I took the prospect while finishing my senior year at Azusa Pacific University and organized/managed a team of 14. I spent countless days and nights working insane hours and trying to maintain a high GPA.

My mentor at the time was the host of the show and I looked up to him. Like all my previous mentors, he was someone with expertise in the entertainment field. He promised my team and me that we would be paid for our work after we helped him get the TV show going. I did not know at the time that I was in for a roller coaster with this project. Things were running smooth, until I started watching him close business deals. He made a lot of promises that he could not keep to my team and me. He took advantage of my good nature and the commitment of my team, manipulated situations, and compromised his morals and values for personal gains.

After dealing with this situation for a year and a half, I learned one extremely valuable lesson: always trust your gut. Rather than questioning your decisions or thoughts, be sure and know that you possess all the right answers for yourself. It can be a little difficult to decipher a good mentor from a bad mentor because intentions can be disguised. I've learned the easiest ways to tell if they are genuine are through their morals, values, and actions.

Instead of sitting down and wondering how I was going to pick myself up and trust another mentor, I continued to network. I reached out to mentors and friends that I knew I could trust and they gave me the opportunity to attend a show taping of America's Funniest Home Videos. At the show taping I was asked to play a game with the host of the television show, Tom Bergeron, by one of the producers. Before I could play the game, the production coordinator confused me with someone else and I never had the chance to play the game. To my surprise, the main producer came to me and apologized for the confusion. He said, "I am so sorry that this happened to you, we would love to have you come back and play the game with Tom Bergeron at a different show taping. Can I have your email?"

With confidence I took the bold chance and said, "Better yet, do you have any job openings? I want to work here." The producer was dumbfounded and responded with, "Let's see what we can do, let me take your email and I will reach out to you." To my surprise, the producer kept his word and our relationship developed. I took the opportunity that the universe had presented and walked confidently into the future of my career.

Since that day my journey into Hollywood has broadened and I continue to network. I've always been a firm believer that we meet people throughout our lives for a reason and each encounter comes with valuable lessons to be learned.

Ultimately, through my experiences, I've learned that networking smart means you must work hard, show confidence, and be patient. I gained mentors who invested their time, energy, and advice into my dreams. As a mentee, it is important to be persistent with reaching out, keep up to date with each mentors' lives, soak in their experiences, and learn from their mistakes. And, don't forget, a part of networking is giving back. Make yourself available as a mentor to someone else. It's important to give back to others and teach them what we've acquired in life.

TWEETABLE

To find your networking skills one must remain positive and true to oneself. Do not be afraid of rejection and follow your dreams. #network

*Andria Schultz is the CEO/Founder of Network Smart and her Brand **Andria Schultz**, which focuses on her passion of helping millennial's get their foot into the entertainment industry by learning through the eyes of executives, celebrities, and professionals behind the scenes. Andria's goal is to inspire all ages to go after their dreams and not be afraid of rejection. Connect at www.networksmart.co, www.andriaschultz.com, Instagram: AndriaCSchultz or email: andriaschultznetworksmart@gmail.com or acschultz09@gmail.com*

Fat, Fatigued, and Frazzled to Fitness Competitor

By Zina Solomon

Like many young girls, I struggled with body image. I felt this pressure of not fitting in with the crowd. Most of the girls were skinny and had a great physique; whereas I was more on the heavy side. The highest I weighed was 150 pounds when I was in my mid-teens.

Being the oldest of six siblings (three of which are also girls), a typical dinner would consist of mac 'n cheese and hot dogs. With a large family, my parent's priority was cost effectiveness not quality or healthy eating. As a result, growing up I was chubby and I hated it. I struggled with having a heavier lower body, thick thighs and big hips. I felt fat, fatigued, and was definitely frazzled. I wanted to do sports but my parents couldn't afford it. I felt trapped and was angry.

I had these thoughts swirling in my head about how life wasn't fair, why me, and how come the other girls have a great body? That inner voice was so loud that I took drastic actions to lose weight, like starving.

I started to take a close look at my health when I was in my sophomore year of college. I paid a visit to a nutritionist who assisted me with portion and timing of meals. That was my first introduction to eating 5-6 small meals per day. I was addicted to diet sodas and my nutritionist suggested that I gradually wean myself off of it. I remember what it was like. It felt like an agonizing experience. That voice again showed up and I felt my resistance rise against following the program as it was designed. However, I took it one day at a time and I joined a gym and started running and weight training.

A turning point in my fitness journey took place when my father passed away when I was 19 years of age. He was 54 years young. He had pancreatic and abdominal cancer. It had spread and after multiple surgeries he did not make it. At that moment it was so clear to me that health was everything and without honoring our bodies we don't get to experience life. I made a commitment to myself that I would be and stay healthy and that I would help others do the same. One way I quieted that inner voice was creating a vision and a goal bigger than myself and committing to achieving it.

One of the things that I dreamed of doing was a fitness competition. In October 2014, I made the decision to compete and transform my body (i.e. take my fitness game to a whole new level). I got on a specific meal and workout plan, but struggled with sticking to it. My old habit muscles were much more trained than what I had set out to do. I fell into the habit of eating 3-4 meals, without the right macronutrients, and wasn't training at least 6 days a week. I struggled with sticking to the plan because that resistance and inner voice showed up again.

Competing was a new process for me. The voice in my head was telling me how hard, uncomfortable, and scary this was. I resisted and didn't trust the process. I felt like I wasn't good enough to compete and I convinced myself I didn't have a great body. I also feared being vulnerable on stage. Going out in a bikini on stage in front of hundreds or thousands of people definitely takes courage. I feared being exposed.

Resistance was in the way of me competing sooner than 2016. I was going to compete in 2015 but bailed out 2 weeks before the show because I freaked out. I was masking my insecurity, with words and attention of others. Don't get me wrong, I had a very supportive group of women who were on the same path as I was. But, my internal dialogue (inner chatter) with myself did not support my dream of competing. Most of my resistance was taking place internally. I was listening to that voice and trusting it instead of honoring it, quieting it down, and trusting the process.

I realized on this journey that I was trying to figure things out on my own and was not really listening to the experts. I felt like I must know better. I know it isn't fun being a lone wolf who is working so hard to figure things out instead of focusing on the task at hand. I was left with the experience of feeling exhausted and disempowered.

After I bailed out on my November 2015 show in Las Vegas, I decided that I was going to take myself and my commitment seriously. I decided to stop resisting and surrender to the process. My first step was recognizing that inner voice and truly listening to others' words of encouragement. I relied on my coach and my friends, who formerly competed, for advice. They were very supportive and they were there for me every step of the way. I practiced my posing and stage presence. I checked in weekly with my coach and held myself accountable to being open and honest with how I was feeling and what was going on. Quieting that voice created a space for me to actually focus on performing (training and preparing meals).

I also stopped taking the whole process so seriously. Fun was definitely missing. I'm all about having fun and I had a choice on how I was going to go through this journey. I was either going to struggle or have fun with it. I chose the latter.

Fitness Universe Miami Beach June 2016 was truly a magical experience. From hair to makeup to spray tanning to theme wear. When my number was called my heart was pounding. I was so nervous and I actually messed up my posing routine on my first round. A few months prior I would have allowed my inner voice to say "OMG. I look like an idiot." However, I kept my composure and as soon as I walked off stage I reminded myself I did it!

It was an exhilarating experience. I could have let that inner voice harm and hinder my journey, but I didn't. If I had, I would have never done my workouts, done my meal plans, or competed for that matter. Transforming that voice into positive thoughts and visualization reinforced what I had set to accomplish. It wasn't easy, but it was absolutely worth it.

Here are my tips for addressing and transforming that voice telling you that you can't. You can!

1. Decide. Commit. Succeed. The first step in creating transformation is being willing to transform, choosing, and deciding to do it. Once you're clear on your commitment, you'll quiet that voice and focus on taking those actions aligned with your commitment.

2. Release Resistance. We all have some form of resistance that shows up between where we are now and where we want to be (i.e. our dreams). Your inner voice is a form of resistance. Recognize what that resistance looks like for you then release it and let it go. Give it up. It no longer serves you. You'll discover that by being courageous enough to release resistance you'll be free and you'll create the space to give back and assist others.

3. Trust Yourself & Others for Support. You will NOT know all the answers on your journey and the idea is that you shouldn't. Allow people to contribute to you. Trust the magic of the process and allow yourself to have fun. Listen to your greatness and not that inner voice.

4. Be Authentic. You want to be honest with yourself on what you truly want in life and what goals you want to create. Be insightfully straight and vulnerable with your dreams and passions in life. We only live once on this earth plane. When you are true to yourself you live a fulfilled and happy life. You'll feel accomplished and you'll be able to serve others.

TWEETABLE
Trust your supportive inner voice not your inner bully.
#Passionista #InnerVoice #SIYC #InspiredEnterpreneur

Zina Solomon is a coach, actress, fitness competitor, co-author, mediapreneur, and social media ninja. She is passionate about making a difference. She assists her clients with achieving results in life, fitness, and business. Connect at www.zinasolomon.com/Connect

Going from Not Knowing Anyone to Having Over 200 Successful Entrepreneurs, Investors and Mentors on Your Squad Is Easier Than You Think!

By Justyna Kedra and Parvathi Mukundan

The crossroads of entrepreneurship and passion is both an unknown and incredibly exciting territory. The opportunity to take your passion and make a living out of it is something that many people seek in life. It's especially rewarding when you're able to create something of value, make money, and help others along the way. But, like a lot of the good stuff in life, it's often "easier said than done."

When you set off on your own journey, it's a road that comes with a lot of hard work, dedication, and resilience. When they say that it takes a village… They mean it! But how do you go from having an idea to having a business? Our advice? Build your own village!

That's where the idea of WE Rule was born in the midst of two twenty-something year olds' need for connections, mentors, and a helping hand in the world of entrepreneurialism. Today, WE Rule is a global community of female entrepreneurs, mentors, and investors who are on a mission to build successful, lasting, and diverse businesses. On our personal career journeys we discovered the demand to create our own networks in order to find success and, through this, found our passion for helping others do the same. Building our platform has not been easy, but we know that we have opened the door to helping more modern day entrepreneurs find their village, and it is only growing bigger and stronger!

Parvathi: The early stage of the ideas and concepts behind WE Rule were formed right in our living room. After a long day of working on my graduate school projects and job applications, I would come home, plop down on our big comfy couch in our New York City apartment and listen to Justyna share stories about some of the friends that she had interviewed in the very initial stages. Our late night roommate conversations quickly turned into brainstorm sessions of sharing ideas, forming plans, and coming up with strategies to take the platform to the next level. After weeks of discussing how we needed our own connections, we were talking about building a network for women across the nation.

It was natural that we started working together—we both share an interest in entrepreneurship, helping others, and sharing stories. Moreover, Justyna has such a positive, upbeat energy that makes it a blast to work with her. What started as an Instagram account has expanded to an online platform full of good vibes and inspiration. The audience reach grew exponentially— from our humble beginnings in New York to nationally across the US and eventually, expanding globally. The stories of each entrepreneur began to weave together and we were beginning to see an amazing narrative.

Regardless of the industry, size, or reach we began to see trends and commonalities. On the journey towards building their village, women were looking for funding and a support system or network to take their business to the next level. We have only scratched the surface of the potential for the platform. We have come such a long way in a year and feel so incredibly grateful and excited about what the future holds.

Justyna: What's so funny about all of this is that, the first year or so, we lived together and didn't even know each other. Through connecting and sharing our ideas about the millennial career struggle we went from "hi/bye" and being strangers to expanding the platform globally. If you think about starting a business and getting a business partner—look around first! The perfect person might be already next to you!

Eventually, we went on to bring on contributors and share our concept with partners at Venture Capital firms from New York and Chicago to Switzerland, Poland, Australia (and counting) to see if they would even consider partnering with us in the future. Their responses have always been "Yes, let us know when you are ready to start the funding process!" That's a pretty big jump in one year, huh? I believe the start of building my own village and the creation of a platform for women across the globe started the day Parvathi and I connected on our ideas. That's what happens when you share your ideas with others, put some good vibes into the universe, and get to work.

Building a business truly takes a village of two or five or more. It's important for us to keep on building our community and developing personal relationships with successful entrepreneurs and investors as well as incubators and organizations that help women on a more local scale. *We don't want to compete, but we do want to connect.*

And, WE Rule is all about connecting but not in the "old-school" way. Everyone tells you to reach out to people who inspire you and ask them out for coffee. That works, but we felt there had to be a way for us to meet successful people while also having something to offer in return for their super valuable time. We knew that female business owners needed their voice to be heard and we wanted their advice, so, we decided to create a platform, where they could share their unique stories. We found this exchange increased our chances of them agreeing to a meeting or a phone call, so we got to work and started connecting. Always think creatively about how to engage with people! Stand out from the crowd and the right people will come your way.

WE Rule connects the world and makes it a better place for female entrepreneurs—no matter where they are right now or where they came from. As two young entrepreneurs, we believe everyone should have access to a powerful network, capital, and the ability to take their business to the next level, purely based on their profitability and ability to grow—nothing more and nothing less.

Our goal is to become the biggest index of female-owned businesses in the world. The dream is to become the first resource that comes to mind for any female business owner globally who is looking to network digitally and searching for funding (at whatever stage that may be). We want to bring everyone together, connect the dots, and close the gap once and for all—all online.

Through this incredible journey there are several things that we have learned that are imperative for personal and professional growth of any individual—millennial or not. These are pointers that we learned along the way and it would be helpful for anyone starting their own entrepreneurial journey who is unsure how to go about it.

Key Takeaways:
• You can't do it alone.
• Don't underestimate your current resources.
• Don't wait. Just go for it.

First, there is no need to go on this mission all alone. It's important to have a support system and network that is able to provide guidance and advice. Next, you shouldn't underestimate your current network.There are numerous resources—whether it's people or access to information, well within your reach. It's important to tap into that network and utilize what's right in front of you. And lastly, it's crucial to recognize that there is no need to wait for the right time or place; instead, just jump in and go for it! If you put in work and recognize what your passion is you will find a way to make your dream come true. Different people and experiences will bring unique perspectives that will allow you to look at challenges with a fresh perspective.

Don't wait for tomorrow. Start building today and start thinking long term. Nothing great was ever built in a day, so start looking at what you already have in your life and just begin. With true passion, the right people around you, and hard work you will be able to transform into a true passionista in no time!

TWEETABLE

Dear #Passionistas, building a #successful #business is all about having a #powerful #network! Justyna +Parvathi #founders of @_we.rule

Justyna Kedra and Parvathi Mukundan are founders of WE Rule, a digital global community connecting female entrepreneurs to mentors, investors, business opportunities. They inspire women all over the world and help them grow bigger, better businesses.

If you are an entrepreneur, lost in the world of business, start building your village. Better yet, join WE Rule! Let's make the village bigger and stronger than ever before for us, for you and for future generations.

Connect via we-rule.com.

Who Is Krystaalized

By Marilyn Flores

Reading scripts and memorizing lines has always been difficult for me. Even though I read the script over and over about 10 times, I still wasn't able to get the lines down. I would cry out of the blue not knowing why I wasn't able to memorize lines. About a year ago in 2015, my mother told me that I suffer from dyslexia, a disorder with symptoms that include late talking, learning new words slowly, and a delay in learning to read. Finally the memories of my childhood and why I suffered in school made sense. I researched to see if there is any way to treat it. Unfortunately, I couldn't find the answers. Acting is my passion and I got into a whole confusion about whether it really was for me.

In 2013 I got involved in the dancing industry and began doing video after video of me dancing and posting them on social media. It released the stress of the situations I went through by being cyberbullied. Cyberbullying is a big problem in our generation. I felt that I had to please everyone, but from that I learned that you can not please everyone. No matter what, there will always be those who dislike or disagree with your decisions. When dancing took over, I thought it was something I really wanted to do for the rest of my life. Until I started realizing that I was forgetting the moves. After 20 minutes of learning I wouldn't remember anything. I started putting myself down, thinking I wasn't good enough. I didn't want to do anymore Youtube videos because I was afraid that viewers would judge me.

There I failed; I completely stopped what I was getting known for. I lost my motivation. The news came out about my suffering with dyslexia. I got into depression thinking everyone disliked me. Friendships became tough because everyone who I thought was a friend was only using me because of my social media followings. I didn't know what I wanted to do with my life.

My mother was wondering why I hadn't done anything. She gave me the idea to start my own business if I didn't want to get into the acting world. I got very excited for something new in my life, but acting had always been my career. At that point, I was lost. We agreed to open up a business for me in which I knew nothing at all: a restaurant.

We went into debt. My mother put all her money into the business and yet I was still putting myself down. It took us 8 months to open my new restaurant and I had no idea what to do. Until one day... my mother and I took a break from the city and took a road trip on the 101 freeway of California. There, being in the road, seeing the beach, I thought about everything I wanted to do. "What do I want to be? How will I get to where I want to be? What is my purpose here on earth?" From that trip I realized how blessed I was. I had not realized all the things God had given me. A new restaurant, a good family, and the best mother in the world. How was I so blind to this?

I found my happiness on that road trip. Finally, I said to myself, "Even though I suffer from dyslexia, I will not let that affect me. I am a strong woman and nothing can bring me down."

I then started planning my life. I bought a cardboard poster and started writing my goals, my fears, my future. Soon the restaurant was a success. Now customers come everyday and we make more than expected. I have been working on acting full time and got my new apartment. I got back in the game for social media and have been gaining followers everyday. Bigger opportunities have crossed my path and here I am telling you my story because writing has become a huge influence in my life. I want to let others who suffer from dyslexia know that it is possible to go for your passion. No matter what, just keep practicing everyday. Now I practice everyday and I have success memorizing my lines! Everything just takes time and patience. Not everything is perfect and everything will not be handed to you. No, it doesn't work like that. You have to work hard for it in order to be successful. Going through a challenge is what makes you even stronger. We cannot be weak and try to find a easy way out of it. Life is a blessing for all of us. Take advantage of that.

TWEETABLE

Never give up even on bumpy roads, always have your head up, and keep driving to your destination.
—Krystaalized #passionistas

Actress and social media influencer Marilyn Flores aka Krystaalized started her career as a must-watch dancing Youtuber then gained a loyal following on many social channels, especially Instagram and Facebook. She takes her supporters everywhere, even skydiving, 2 months in Europe, and screenings, red carpets and charity events. Marilyn inspires her peers to never give up on bumpy roads, always have your head up, and keep driving to your destination. Instagram.Facebook.Twitter: @Krystaalized

Photo credit: Jay Jarell

Design Your Life. Shine Your Light. Live Your Dreams

By Kristen Stephens Sharma

Imagine a world where you could not only design your dream life, but also live it. I have a newsflash for you, we live in this world. I am an example of someone who worked hard to live my dream life. I am not talking about planning every action to a tee or living out perfection. I am talking about creating a path of happiness, on which you live out your passions.

I love life. I love MY life because I have designed it. I shine my light and am passionate about the things I choose to do. Because of this, I am living my dreams!

I am one who believes you can have it all, do it all, and experience it all. As an interior designer, real estate investor, artist, inspirational keynote speaker, spa owner, singer/songwriter, success coach, humanitarian and world traveler; I am a passionista.

For nearly 25 years I've lived by the motto—through intentional design, education, passion and love, anything is possible! It took a lot of hard work, but ultimately, living my dream life happened after I made the decision to make it happen.

At the age of 27, after my second son was born, I realized I was bored with my life and struggling with depression. I was dissatisfied. I was a wife, mother, and clerk at the county courthouse living an average life, earning $12.00/hour. I was living a life without sizzle, sparkle, or passion. This pain motivated me, as I knew there was more.

As a child, I did not start in an advantaged position. We were fairly poor. I had buck teeth and was bullied. I was not as academically inclined as my siblings and struggled to get good grades. I never felt "good enough." I dreamed then of the life I live now, but I didn't accept that living it was possible. I didn't know the power was in my hands to design my life.

As I aged, I got braces (thanks Mom and Dad!), became an honors student, was recognized as an All-State vocalist, and won most improved player on the Volleyball team. Once I got a taste of feeling confident and winning, I became inspired. I knew very intimately what it meant to suffer and what it meant to succeed. Succeeding was much more fun! When I got to that low point at 27, I needed that feeling of success again, so I made the decision to design and live my dream life.

My search for more began with a look at my roots. I knew if I wanted to grow more beautiful fruit in my life, I had to check the source, my inner self. I dove into self-help books and audios and became addicted to improving my inner being.

Shortly after, I quit my job to follow my passions (and there were many), which at the time involved raising my two beautiful, young sons and creating artwork, as I was a self-taught artist. Yes, I was terrified, but I knew nothing risked meant nothing gained!

My joy skyrocketed after that decision and I felt alive again. Instead of taking my sons to a daycare, which I disliked, I got to spend my time raising my own children. When they were sleeping or at school, I created custom artwork in my basement; I sold thousands of my pieces around the country.

After my sons (who are grown men now) started attending school full-time, I grew my art business into an interior design consulting business. Within two years, I was making six figures, working only 20 hours a week. I then expanded that into real estate investing and started buying up homes to fix and flip and also rent. While making quite the name for myself, I was having fun and living passionately.

Within a few years, I was honored to take on the role of design consultant for the Deepak Chopra Center for Living in California. I loved the design end of this position, but even more so, I enjoyed the holistic healing aspect of the project. Within one year, I created my own holistic healing school and several holistic healing spa locations. This was possible due to the money I had been saving for years prior, approval for a SBA loan, and my willingness to take a risk on a dream. Not to mention I had a team of amazing experts in the areas of massage, energy healing, aromatherapy, ayurveda, pathology, psychology, anatomy, physiology, Reiki, Tai Chi, meditation and more teaching me and supporting my vision.

As students began pouring in, I found out I was nominated for "Business of the Year" and won. Two years later, I was nominated "Female Entrepreneur of the Year" and won. With a passion for helping others and refusal to live a boring life, I realized I felt best when I was shining my light. I started teaching others what I knew by becoming a Success Coach.

This mindset has allowed me to learn, grow, and experience remarkable things. I have been in the top 5% of female earners in the United States for over 15 years now. I have bought and sold millions of dollars in real estate and have owned 10 successful businesses. I have met and studied with experts and thought leaders including: Tony Robbins, Bob Proctor, Deepak Chopra, Louise Hay, Barbara DeAngelis, Wayne Dyer, Jack Canfield, John Gray, Cheryl Richardson and more. I have been the co-author of several books; one reaching #1 on Amazon. I co-wrote and performed as lead vocalist for the theme song for the California Women's Conference (the largest women's conference in the nation), and I have co-written and sang music with #1 singer/songwriters and Emmy award winners. I have shared the podium with Arianna Huffington, founder of the Huffington Post, and sang the National Anthem in front of 23,000 people, including Michael Jordan and several Gold Medalist Olympians. I have traveled and enjoyed many exotic locations including: riding motorcycles through South Africa, bungee jumping off bridges in Canada, white water rafting through the rivers of Idaho, traveling the Orient Express from Paris to Venice, singing on the Great Wall of China, Eiffel Tower, and at the Taj Mahal, and snorkeling in the Virgin Islands.

As an interior designer, I have learned that I can apply design concepts to life, making it more beautiful. A couple of the ways I have done this for myself over the years, and for others, is to ignite more self awareness through my Dream Life Binder and Life Balance classes. Here's a sneak peek on how these work.....

The Dream Life Binder.
Take a three ring binder you love and create an inspiring front cover for yourself. Then, take several black pieces of cardstock (10-100) and punch three holes in them. Now the fun begins!

Part 1: Go through magazines and online stock photos, and choose images that you love (things you find beautiful, would love to have or experience.) My Dream Life Binder includes photos of my family and those I love, oceans, sunsets, candles, flowers, nature, happy people, beautiful homes, travel destinations, healthy looking women, sexy cars, and more. Glue these printed photos to the stock paper in a way that inspires you.

Part 2: Go to your computer and start typing out phrases, quotes and words that inspire you. Print them out, in a large font, and add 2-5 phrases to each page. By the time you are done, you will essentially have your own Dream Life Binder.

Part 3: Look through the pages of your binder on a regular basis, and allow yourself to "feel the feelings" of having all that you love. Let the photos inspire you. As they become attracted to you, through vibration, they will begin to show up more in your life. (The reason I love a binder instead of a board is because the binder can easily travel with you on your adventures!)

The mission statement in my Dream Life Binder reads: "To inspire myself and others, to use their God given gifts, to heal and enlighten the world, while experiencing love, joy, passion and peace." This mission inspires my life's design.

If you intentionally design your life and follow some basic principles, you can also have a life you love to live. I want to leave you with three pieces of wisdom I have picked up while designing the life I love to live.

1. Believe in yourself! If people tell you you can't, use that as fuel to get you where you want to be. People told Taylor Swift she could not sing. People told Shakira she sounded like a billy goat. People told Jessica Simpson that she was too full-figured to be a fashion mogul. Anything is possible!!

2. Never give up. Some won't agree with you. Some will want to dim your light. Keep shining! No matter what.

3. Innovate. The only thing we can count on is that things will change. Stay with the times. Be sure that what you have to offer is needed in the world. When you help people meet their needs, you will become a shining star.

TWEETABLE

Design Your Life. Shine Your Light. Live Your Dreams. #Shine #SuccessCoaching #InspirationOMG #KristenStephens #AwardWinning

Kristen Stephens Sharma has the recipe for fulfillment and loves success coaching. Her new program, www.InspirationOMG.com,"inspiration for the spunky, spiritual woman," offering free inspirational videos on YouTube, 21-day challenges, eight-week online programs, webinars, mastermind groups, and beautiful island retreats, all to help the spunky, spiritual woman live her dream life, launches January 1st, 2017. Contact: (319)321-2450

www.KristenSharma.com | Kristen@KristenSharma.com

I Chose Magic, Yes Magic

By Mariela Torres

I was laying on the floor looking up at my 16-foot ceiling, feeling lost and stagnant. I had this overwhelming feeling of what the hell am I doing with my life, piercing through every single pore of my body. I had never felt so disconnected than at this very moment. It was the first week of December 2014, and what would follow would be a difficult and life changing series of events.

Let's just say 2015 was the hardest, but best year of my life. My engagement, with a man I had been with for 10 years, ended. I quit my corporate job at Bloomingdales. I moved out of my two story loft in the Gaslamp of downtown San Diego to my parents' home. And, I went from making great money to no money at all. My life had completely changed from one year to another.

Outside looking in, all these bad things were happening, yet I felt so alive. My life had always been so structured. I've lived in the same house all my life. I went to the same school, had the same friends and boyfriend; my entire life was such a routine.

After these initial changes I became obsessed with the unknown. I loved not knowing where life was going to take me. All I knew was what I wanted to do, which was to own a clothing line and online boutique that inspired women. And, I knew who I wanted to become, which was a f**king BOSS. Towards the end of that year, the most difficult life change occurred and my perspective was once again altered.

The event that completely changed my entire life and did the most to put things in perspective, for me, was the passing of my mother. In November of 2015, she passed away from a sudden heart attack. I had already started the clothing line but her passing gave me an extra kick in the cajones. We hear it all the time "life is short" and it's because it's so utterly true.

I started working hard everyday to reach my goals. Today, I'm not nearly close, but as the great Abraham-Hicks once said, "You're always, always, always going to be on your way to something more—always and when you relax and accept that and stop beating up on yourself for not being someplace that you're not, and instead, start embracing where you are while you keep your eye on where you're going—now life becomes really, really, really fun"

Don't get me wrong, I do have somewhat of a daily routine and a bit of structure, which is needed. But now, I have fun with it all. I live in adventure, and I don't get caught up in regimen.

My life changes in 2015 helped me realize life was going to run its course, I had no power over what life was throwing at me, but I had the power to see the magic within the difficult times and embrace it. It wasn't until I chose to see the magic that I became truly happy and successful. I've learned that life shouldn't be so black and white. Throw some color into that shit!

With my newfound perspective, I decided to only focus on building my brand from then on. I would not have a plan B. This gave me such drive. When something tragic happens we have two options: we can let it hinder us or motivate and inspire us. In circumstances like this the only thing we have control over is our reaction to what is happening to the world around us. My advice is to always choose the positive reaction because the negative reaction isn't going to take you anywhere.

It is important to be centered, to feel at peace and at ease. I start my day thanking the universe for everything happening in my life, every situation, good and bad. You have to recognize the bad and keep in mind that hurdles are sent to us to learn, grow, and build character and strength. There are certain things you cannot control, like in my case, my mother passing away.

From this life change, I learned the power of surrendering and how to let life take its course. The more you try to control a situation the more it controls your life. Don't spend energy on shit you can't control. Let it go and trust that the universe has your back. After you recognize the heartbreaks, allow the soul to heal by embracing the amazing moments of life. Choose to find the magic in it all.

Today, I am proud to say that my clothing line, Killem With Chic, is my full time job. The name of my brand came to be after seeing this quote, "CHIC—creating happiness, inspiring confidence." I thought that's the sort of movement I'd like to create. The 'Killem' part added a badass vibe.

With this movement, I am making money doing what I passionately love to do. I have my own place and an amazing workspace/office. I found my soul mate, and I am oh so madly in love. My relationship with my father and brother have never been closer. And, I get to create rad clothing, style up models, have photo shoots, sell awesome clothes online, and make women feel beautiful and empowered.

A year later, I am amazed at where I have taken my brand. I am almost in 10 stores throughout San Diego. I've been featured in magazine articles, and I have had countless collaborations and pop up shops. I was able to showcase on the runway for Fashion Week San Diego in October 2016. Despite the hard times I found the magic by believing in myself and my vision. I knew that the beginning was going to be hard, but I kept in mind that the hard times would pass. I also knew I couldn't give up pursuing what made me feel so alive.

My mother, who I was blessed to have in this world, used to always say, "Start now not tomorrow." Set a goal and choose to see the magic now. Once you make that choice, I promise the universe will conspire to make it happen for you. I hope you live in color!

TWEETABLE
Don't spend energy on shit you can't control! Let it go and trust that the universe has your back! #killem #choosemagic #passionistas

Mariela Torres is founder of Killem With Chic; she's also a designer, stylist, and blogger. She also loves photography and takes most of her pictures for her online store. Her blogs are mainly focused on empowering and inspiring others through her life experiences and spiritual beliefs. She is a messenger of love.

Follow @mariela__t and @killemwithchic

Contact info@killemwithchic.com

Check us out at www.killemwithchic.com

Your Most Important Decision

By Heather Christie

When I was a young attorney, I was on a mission. I was full of energy and ambition to be successful and was searching for a mentor who would help me fall in love with my profession and find my way to the top. I wasn't just looking for any mentor. I was looking for "the" mentor. A role model. A strong female equity partner who was a top notch lawyer with a fabulous husband and kids who also found a way to balance her family, friends and work. My challenge? I couldn't find her.

The truth was, on the inside, I desperately wanted to be an entrepreneur. I was dying for the freedom that comes with entrepreneurship, but I was strapped with six figures in student loans from law school. I felt completely trapped. I found myself living paycheck to paycheck with a little extra stacking up on credit cards each month. My lack of financial mastery at the time had me in a place that required every bit of my six figure income, so I couldn't possibly abandon ship to follow my entrepreneurial dreams.

The real problem: I didn't know what to do or how to do it. More importantly, I didn't have enough belief in myself that I could make the leap from employee to entrepreneur to figure out those first two questions. I didn't have that belief until I met the man on the plane...

Early in 2001, I was boarding an early morning flight from Indianapolis to Chicago. Back in my days when I lived out of a suitcase, I came to cherish my airplane "me" time. No one could find me in my little airplane bubble because this was pre-airplane-wifi. When I approached my seat, my seatmate was already seated, nose deep in his book. I remember thinking nice, no worries about this one talking too much.

As soon as we reached our cruising altitude, my seatmate closed his book with a dramatic sigh. Oh crap, I said to myself, he wants to tell me about his book. My airplane bubble was just about to be compromised. He turned to me, handed me the book and slowly and emphatically said to me, "Here, this book is for you. You're going to need it. It's going to change your life." That was it. Nothing more.

I accepted the book, looked at the title and thought, "*Rich Dad Poor Dad,* that sounds ridiculous." However, I could not mistake his genuine sincerity that this book was meant for me and was going to change my life. His authentic belief in me made me believe in myself—I call it "borrowed belief." Have you ever noticed that it is easier to believe in someone else's belief in you than to believe in yourself? The borrowed belief was just enough to get me started.

At 30,000 feet in the air, I opened the book and started reading. Before I knew it, the flight attendants were instructed by the captain to prepare the cabin for landing. I was nose deep in that book just as my seatmate had been. So much so, that I continued reading during the 45 minute cab ride from O'Hare back to my place in the city.

When I got home, I shed my suitcase and briefcase in the foyer, sat down on my couch in the family room, and continued to read the book from cover to cover. I suspect that I had a similar sigh as my benefactor did when I closed the book. Game changer!

While reading that book, I realized that somewhere along the line, I had suspended using the most powerful asset I had in life—my mind. I'm not sure when it happened or how it happened. My guess is that it occurred when I finished law school. I had subconsciously accepted the notion that when I finished school, I was done learning and it was off to work.

After that light bulb went off and my mind was engaged, I was able to uncover my epiphany. For years, I had the mistaken belief that it was up to someone else, someone in my law firm, to grow and mentor me. I thought it was someone else's role to develop me and teach me how to move to the next level.

Finally, I discovered that my results in life, all of my success in life, was a measure of my personal and professional growth. My relationships, my health and fitness, my financial success was a reflection of my personal and professional growth. If I was waiting for someone else to develop me, then I was on someone else's watch for all the results in my life. Why on earth would I want to let anyone else (other than me) dictate the amount of success that I would have in my life?

After these discoveries, I made a decision that would prove to completely alter the direction of my life for the rest of my life. The most important decision of my career. My decision: I take full personal responsibility for all of my success and results in my life and I am fully committed to being a lifelong learner. I vowed to attend seminars, read books, watch videos, and learn from everyone I encountered so that I would continuously grow and develop. It was this commitment to my own development that ultimately gave me the courage to quit my job (after making partner) and follow my entrepreneurial passion.

Whether I am sharing this story with a live audience of 30 or 300, undoubtedly people tell me they can't wait to get their hands on that book! What if I were to tell you just as I have told other executives around the world it wasn't just that book that changed my life? What if it was the mindset that I had when I read the book? It was the borrowed belief from my seatmate that the book would change my life that helped me to make the decision that actually changed my life. How many times have you read a great book, but failed to decide to implement the strategies that you came up with while you read the book?

The word "decide" comes from the Latin word that means literally "to cut off." When I made the decision to take personal responsibility for my personal and professional growth, I literally cut off my uncertain future and replaced it with a future that was filled with growth, change, and success.

All action in life is preceded by a decision. I began taking actions in a different way after I made that decision. The book, *Rich Dad Poor Dad*, was the catalyst. The day that I was given that gift—the best gift that I have ever opened—I believe that I was also given the responsibility to share it with others. The gift that I opened that day was not just the book. The gift that I opened that day was my mind.

The day that I made that decision is the day that I got "on the court" of my life. I chose to develop me. As Jim Rohn said, "work harder on yourself than you to on your job." On the court, I take personal responsibility for all my successes and failures in life. That is very different from being "off the court" where I was filled with complaints about my debt and my job and blamed my circumstances for my results in life. I made excuses for my lack of personal growth—like not having a mentor. Where are you making excuses that are keeping you where you are in life?

From my experience over the last 12 years, coaching hundreds of individuals, I know that you have a decision to make that will help you evolve to the next level. A decision that will help you to find or follow your passion. Do you know what that decision is right now? If so, I challenge you to write it down and get committed. It doesn't matter right now if you don't know what to do or how to do it. Make the decision and commit to developing an action plan.

Remember, change starts with a decision. There is only one thing in this life over which you have full control—it is the power to control and direct your mind toward whatever you want. Make a decision right now about what you want and go after it. Don't stop until you find it!

TWEETABLE

#Decide to develop yourself. Engage your mind. No one else will. —Heather Christie #OnTheCourt #LifelongLearner #Passionistas

Heather Christie is a Master Executive and Leadership Coach, Professional Speaker, Published Author and "Recovering Attorney." She primarily speaks to Leadership Groups within Corporations and Industry Trade Associations. Connect at: heatherchristie.com or email heather@heatherchristie.com.

Channeling Your Inner Badass

By Carlisle Studer

When trying to channel your inner badass fear is the worst possible "F-word" I can think of, seriously. How many times a day do you hesitate, question yourself, or just plain avoid a situation because of this crippling emotion we call fear? Often your imagination can take one tiny negative thought and turn it into a terrifying mind takeover.

My trick to living a fearless life is channeling the right character for the situation. I have been an actress for eleven years now and have worked as an acting coach to young kids for the past three. My favorite part of books and movies has always been the colorful or mysterious characters that star in them.

In middle school, I was envious of the teenage girls, who were professional spies, in one of my favorite books. Naturally as an actress, I decided to take all of the things I had learned about being a spy in the book and apply it to my everyday life. With "gadgets" in my purse, I would count the number of possible exits when I walked into a room, and I would often eavesdrop on other people's conversations listening for "clues." Luckily for me, playing pretend was actually my career and dream. Acting gave me the tools to channel characters that were fearless.

I will never forget my first day of eighth grade. Growing up homeschooled, I had never attended a real school, until that year. I walked into the school building, holding my summer projects and new Hello Kitty book bag that I was very proud of. I remember feeling very anxious and small. All of the other kids were hugging each other and exchanging summer stories. I had no clue who anyone was or where any of my classes were. In that moment fear had paralyzed me and I began to rethink my entire decision of going to a real school. Then I decided to do what I do best, to act my way through it.

I decided to channel the role of Blair Waldorf from *Gossip Girl* TV show. Blair was fearless and studious, which was everything I needed to be in that moment. Pulling my shoulders back and putting a smirk on my face I walked forward confidently to find my first class. Using my acting skills to embody a character helped me get through the first few weeks of school.

A few months later, that school began to feel like home, and now I had stories to share with the friends I had made.

Fast forward six years and I am sitting passenger seat driving through El Paso on my way to Los Angeles. The city of angels had been calling my name my whole life, and I could not wait for the moment I became old enough to go be an actress in Los Angeles. Looking out the window passing through Texas, I was telling my dad all of my plans and goals for the New Year and my new life.

Moving into my first apartment felt electric, I could see palm trees outside my window and it felt like home. After the initial excitement of moving to a new city faded away, that tiny antagonist in my head started posing questions like "Would it have just been best if you stayed home?" Or "How do you expect to be successful when everyone else in LA is an actor too?" I began to take these questions seriously.

Meetings posed a challenge. Many would make sarcastic comments such as "Let me guess…you're here to be a star right?" This fueled this small fear fire that I had started in my head.

I started to feel shame and inadequacy when I would tell them I was an actor. Fear prompted me to laugh it off and reply with "Oh you know, just like everyone else here I want to be in movies!" I continued to do this for weeks until one day I had an epiphany, while talking to this stranger in line at Starbucks.

Los Angeles is just a bigger pond than I'm used to. Why do I care what this stranger thinks of me? I discovered this fear was coming from a place of not feeling "good enough" to live in this huge city and be successful.

From that moment on I decided to channel a total badass character, as I had succeeded to do in many other life changes. This character was CONFIDENTLY pursuing her dreams; this character was not ashamed of who she was and what she loved. After I made the choice I felt invincible in the face of any situation. Now, the moment I begin to feel fear creeping up on me, I take a second, and use my acting skills to make me feel fearless. And yes, at first it is a "fake it until you make it" mindset but then, fearlessness became a habit.

Any new task, dream, or adventure in life can feel very intimidating and at times completely terrifying. In that time before venturing out into the unknown, there is a chance to leave all doubt behind. Outsmarting fear just takes a little bit of acting skills and a good imagination.

Here are my tips for channeling your inner badass:

1. Choose a character from a movie or book, who you believe can handle any situation.

2. Take a breath and think about what that character would do.

3. Go forth confidently, using this character as a mask for your fear or doubt.

4. Use this newfound confidence and courage everyday, it is now a new "muscle" of yours, so it likes to be worked!

5. Dress like the character you wish to channel. I have always believed that a good pair of heels can make a woman feel powerful.

Now, it's time to go be your own action hero and kick fear right in the a**! HA!

TWEETABLE

Make facing your fears fun, use it as a challenge, or an opportunity for a funny story.
—Carlisle Studer #freedomisfearless #passionistas

Carlisle Studer is a poetry lover and actress whose mission is to positively impact the entertainment industry. Growing up an actress, Carlisle learned the best way to begin a success journey is by facing your fears. Launching her career as an adult in Los Angeles, she also found a love for live improvisational performance. Carlisle uses her acting and improv skills in everyday life to spread joy and build her brand. Connect with Carlisle on twitter and instagram at @carlislediana

How Fashion Blogging Saved My Life

By Maria Von Losch

After nine years of being together and recently celebrating our six years of marriage on a romantic vacation in Belize, my husband decided that we shouldn't be married anymore. No warning signs, no talks of divorce, ever. Sure we had challenges throughout our marriage, but I never thought we would get divorced. For him, it was over. No marriage counseling, nothing. It wasn't over for me. I was devastated.

Unfortunately, the place we resided in was his place before I met and married him, and he wasn't budging. I had no choice but to pack up and move in with my mom, a two-hour drive down the coast. Honestly, I don't remember much. The first two months after this happened was a blur. I felt hopeless and couldn't see any light down the dark dingy tunnel. Trying to find the positive in why this happened seemed impossible.

While in my divorce coma, it soon hit me that I had binge shopped... a lot. It was evident by the massive decline of my bank balance. I remember thinking Is this really happening to me? What the heck is going on here? Is this my life? What am I going to do now?

As I struggled to deal with my broken heart, my poor mother had to witness my depressed behavior on a daily basis. I was so numb and checked out, staying in my PJ's who knows how many days in a row. Online shopping became my friend because I didn't have to change out of my PJ's into actual clothing.

On the days I managed to get out of my mom's house, I was like a zombie, strolling through the aisles of Nordstrom Rack and Home Goods. Instead of feeding off of brains, I was feeding off of shoes, jewelry, dresses, nail polish, fancy bedding, pillows and pretty much anything stylish in my eyes.

I woke up in panic one morning. Something finally snapped me into reality. I think my natural survival mode kicked in. I needed to see how much money I had in my account. I thought it would be around $1,300? Nope. Oh-em-gee. My draw dropped when my eyes focused in on $130. That's it?! That's all I have? Uh oh.

At this moment of clarity, I woke up. Finally, I was fully present. I thought here I am at 40, no work presently to provide an income because I moved to a new city and no husband for support. I had no choice but to let go of my pride and ask for help from my mom, but I also felt this urgency to do something big, crazy and public.

I had already been blogging about style, beauty and lifestyle for a couple years, so I decided to write about my experience. But, what would I share? I knew I couldn't shop because I had no money and no job prospects. I was slowly working my way back into personal styling for clients and sharing savvy tips about style and shopping. That's it!

I had the idea of shopping my own closet and blogging about it. But for how long? Thirty days, sixty days, ninety days or six months? Not challenging enough. I made the commitment of 365 days, one entire year of no shopping any fashion whatsoever. It was a challenge!

Once I launched this project and made a big public announcement all over my social media, I received such positive feedback. People I hadn't spoken to in years and some I didn't know at all shared their personal stories with me. Little did I know, I was creating a movement.

Four to five months into my challenge, my life got very busy. From being a cast member on a new reality dating show, to networking to meeting and mingling with new friends, to cultivating new relationships with work and projects, and dating post-divorce, my life had changed.

Things and exciting events left me barely anytime to write my blog. Some days I would plan out five to seven outfits and shoot all my photos at once. Then edit and upload to my blog so they were ready to go. Most nights I would try to finish my daily blog entry by midnight but sometimes I was up until 2 a.m. Then, I would take time to share everything on all my social media. Some people asked me if I ever slept. I didn't.

As new seasons of fashion came out, I did have moments when I wanted to buy something new. It was hard to stay relevant with seasonal trends, shopping my own closet. Styling and reworking pieces to make outfits of the day look fresh was a challenge. My audience loved it, however, because I would link back to all the days I reworked one piece. They could see how purchasing smart investment pieces can be styled many different ways. Another challenge that popped up was being exposed to basically anyone who had internet and stumbled upon my blog.

My blog shared deep, emotional and painful moments throughout the year of my shopping project. This left the door open for haters with judgment. That was new for me. I left the negative comments up with my reply saying,"Thanks for reading my blog and sorry you feel that way, but I appreciate the comment." I figured I should stay neutral, kind and diplomatic. Of course, they never responded back.

An amazing thing that arose from this year-long challenge was the positive comments from my loyal readers. I had no idea I would start a movement of some sort. I had a cheering squad of women all around the world, which was very inspiring. This kept me going in moments when I wanted to quit, and trust me, there were moments.

I had some women say how they felt like they were on my journey with me and how some days my entries would make them cry and other days make them laugh. I even had a husband leave a comment once. I'll paraphrase from my memory, something like, "My wife reads your blog every night, and I'm always curious as to what she's reading. I started reading your blog over her shoulder. Now I see why, I'm not a woman but I can see the appeal."

The last month, the final 30-days of my Shop My Closet Challenge, I decided to post a quick outfit video, along with my daily blog post. This was my countdown. It was exciting and people were chiming in everyday. It was like running a marathon but for one entire year!

When my final day arrived on July 7th, I realized not only had I accomplished this year-long goal, but I made an impact in the city I was living in. A good majority of people knew who I was, especially since I had made appearances on the local morning news, talking about style savvy and also about my challenge.

This experience showed me the power in making the best out of a bad situation. Even though I felt I had hit rock bottom, I found the strength and courage to move forward, by making something out of the changes I experienced. I worked through each day, despite feeling lost and uncomfortable at times. Finding that last flicker of fire in the pit of my stomach helped me ignite a new awakening for my life. Doing so, I found success, new passions and happiness. This is how fashion blogging saved my life.

When life has beaten you down and you feel like there's no hope, the best way to get out of this state is to not isolate yourself even if you feel like that's the only alternative. It's all about contrary action. What you "feel" like doing, do the opposite. This has been a lifesaver for me. Remember feelings aren't facts, they're just feelings and they come and go. "We're meant to grow so we have something to give." — Tony Robbins

TWEETABLE

Stop beating yourself up over the things that aren't, be grateful for the things that are.
—Maria Von Losch #passionistas

Maria Von Losch is a life & style expert, digital content creator, social influencer, and media personality. With her creative talents she brings brands to life through styling, photography, writing, and videos. Maria regularly appears on TV as a life & style expert and promoting her experience of shopping her closet for 365 days. The "Shop My Closet" book is coming soon.

Website: savvynista.com / Facebook.Instagram. Pinterest @savvynista / Twitter @mariavonlosch / youtube.com/savvynista.

The Flame Within You That Burns

By Carol Shockley

What is your passion? What is it that sparks the fire within you? Have you been asked these questions while you were in the discovery mode of where your life was headed? I remember back 6 years ago when I started the journey of being an entrepreneur. I found that this was a personal development journey as much as it was a journey to inspire and change the world.

Along this journey I learned a lot about myself as an individual: what inspires me, who I am, where I want to be in life, and what matters most to me. I went on a journey of discovery. I was raised in a controlling environment under a legalistic religion with lots of rules. As I've experienced the world, I've learned how to be me, released from judgment, and to live a life without boundaries.

How we view life matters. How we view others matters. How we talk to ourselves matters. How we love matters. How we listen matters. How we deal with the overwhelm matters. I found what matters most is taking one lesson at a time. There are times when I am overwhelmed and I shut down from life, business, friends, and myself. I tend to do this when I am tackling all the faults I think I have, all the mistakes I think I've made, and I am trying to change it all at once.

I learned that entrepreneurship is a journey. Envision the end in mind first and watch it evolve as you step into it.

I remember back in the fall of 2010 when I met my first coach to be. I started with this idea of the One Thing. The One Thing was going to be a book and I was going to be a speaker. I have notes from back then and I knew at the time that wasn't sparking anything inside of me except for overwhelm. I was forcing myself to do something that didn't drive me.

While I started this journey I was still working with a corporate speaker as his personal assistant. We had a show on the Vegas strip for six months. I managed his schedule and travel throughout the country and I managed the show on the strip—from the box office, the volunteers, the sound team, to the merchandise sales, and our weekly guest performers. One day, my coach had a need for an event planner, which I thought I was far from being, but I knew I loved managing the back of room sales and understood how valuable it was for it to be managed, so I sent a message volunteering my services while he found his next event planner.

Whoa and behold, I walked into my exuberance! I was on fire for five days straight and there was no shutting the energy down. Wow, I now understood the questions, "What's your passion?" "What sparks a fire within you?" and had the answers.

I am an event planner. I love every aspect of creating the relationships, organizing the details, leading the team, and especially being the puppet master pulling the strings. What a whirlwind. Still, that was just the beginning of the discovery. There is a lot more that begins there too.

The next discovery was that I have an opinion and so does everyone else and the coaches. I had to learn the next four primary steps for myself: 1. To LISTEN to my inner voice 2. To TRUST my inner voice 3. To FOLLOW my inner voice 4. To Take ACTION. These four steps never lead me astray. It still amazes me to know that the universe really aligns with my inner self to make the best happen for my life.

A few road bumps usually occur on the journey and I have been tempted to head down another path. It is those times that I have to respond quickly to the presentation and trust my gut. One of those times the opportunity came from a dear friend/mentor via a phone call. I had just returned home from an event and she called asking if I could be ready in 2 hours to jump on a plane to help her for the remainder of the week. I immediately said yes and it just so happened I had a suitcase loaded to go. The details were vague, but I knew she always had my best interests in mind.

The next call I received was from a travel agent that gave me an hour to arrive at the airport. I had scheduled a ride anticipating this call and off I went. I arrived at the airport, boarded the plane, and enjoyed the conversation to follow. The gentlemen and his wife next to me were on their way back home to Toronto and asked me if I was on business or pleasure. I answered, business, and they asked where I was staying, I said I was unsure, they asked who was picking me up and I said I was unsure, they asked how long I was staying and I said I was unsure. I laughed thinking how crazy my answers were, yet I knew I was in the right place at the right time and I was excited about it. The next 6 months were a rollercoaster of excitement and adventure.

Once I arrived in Toronto, there was a driver there waiting and he drove me to the Four Seasons downtown. I met my girlfriend who started to fill me in on my assignment... ready for this!? I was going to assist the Real Wolf on Wall Street, Jordan Belfort. His assistant had just walked out and they had an immediate need. I thought, "Very cool, sure I can do this."

JB and I hit it off when I showed up and was able to manage the Power Point as he dictated changes during a drive to an event. At the end of the week instead of flying back to Vegas I went off to LA with him. I stayed another few days onsite and JB offered me the opportunity to be his personal assistant for an international tour schedule. Again following my intuition, I agreed and started immediately. We toured Ireland, Germany, all across Australia, New Zealand, India, and London. I was living the dream of travel and seeing sights I had at once only imagined. I have made a lot of friends across these parts and enjoyed seeing the countryside. When it ended, off I went to Oklahoma to visit my daughter who was expecting my first grandchild.

Then, another shift occurred and back to event planning I went, though this time with immense knowledge of large productions and behind the scenes. We had events from 1000 to 4000 while I was across the waters working with JB. I was simply amazed by all I had learned and the value I could bring to my own business.

Today, I work with many different entrepreneurs and business owners to bring their vision to life. We impact thousands of lives and businesses every weekend. I work with celebrities and their assistants and I've come to understand the roles each of us play. These relationships matter and knowing your role in business matters too.

When I go back to the questions from the beginning of this story: What is your passion? What is it that sparks the fire within you? I can answer knowing I am forever emerging and that every experience adds to the value I offer the world. I love serving alongside brilliance and impacting the lives of thousands with events.

My clients themselves are experts in their own areas and to name a few: Todd Herman, Ryan Moran, Mike Rayburn, Keith Yackey, Casey Eberhart, Craig Duswalt, Kelly O'Neil, Kirsten Roberts, John Logar, Larry Broughton and the list goes onward. The honor of running events has its bonuses including working with a few celebrities that make an impact: Glenn Morshower, Gary Vaynerchuk, Dean Cain, Kevin Cronin, Duff McKagan, Robert Herjavec, and Jeff Hoffman just to name a handful. Their stories and business knowledge change the world.

Your gifts are ones that come naturally. They are ones you overlook for the natural ability you have in performing them. It surprises me still that others may not like all the details, or pulling the strings, or managing multiple activities at one time and that they don't desire the responsibility. We are all wired differently and there is no right or wrong. Every time an event door opens my eyes light up and flames begin to burn again and again. Know you were created for just this moment in time for the purpose that springs to life within you.

TWEETABLE
Calmness from chaos all begins with trusting your inner voice. —Carol Shockley #eventplanner #createcalmness #managechaos #passionistas

Carol Shockley, founder of Shockley Event Management, creates calm from chaos throughout the planning, strategy and management of simple and complex events. She supports her clients' needs and vision every step of the way, sticks to the budget, and creates the events of their dreams. She takes extra steps to understand the relationship between the event host and attendees to best support the intended outcome.

Contact Carol at www.Shockleyeventmanagement.com or carol@shockleyeventmanagement.com

Operation Why: The Path to Healthy Expectations

By Bethney Bonilla

What if I could tell you your destiny. Would you want to know? If I said I could give you the ultimate playbook to success would you take it?

I'd assume you are thinking *well, duh.*

Many of us spend years, if not decades or lifetimes, seeking passion, dream jobs and the pathway to success. We ponder the who, what, when, where and how. And, most of the advice successful people have to offer involves one of those five factors.

While those topics are worthwhile, I found along my journey they were not enough. I discovered I'd been overlooking the most important factor the *why*.

For years, I'd forgotten to look at the purpose behind my goals and expectations. Taking the time to do this and reframe those intentions helped me to get to where I am today.

My discovery occurred in the summer of 2015, after my college graduation. I decided to move home to the Central Valley of California, leaving the vibrant city of Los Angeles. After a successful and thoroughly planned out college career, I faced the ambiguity of the future, and this terrified me. The worst part was the feeling of unmet expectations, brought about by my worst critic, myself.

From a young age, I was motivated to not only meet but also exceed expectations. High expectations followed me from grade school to graduate school and from my small hometown to across the globe. I believed setting a high bar was the best way to keep my ambition strong and my mind focused. In many instances this worked. That was, until I graduated college and had yet to find my dream job.

Upon my return home, I moved into the bedroom of my four year-old niece. I vividly remember deciding where to stack my books among her toys, boxes of color crayons and piles of stuffed animals.

In my initial days home, I struggled with optimism. I planned to find work, save money and gain experience, while applying to graduate school. I told myself I would take time to enjoy my family and self-reflect. But, my spirit was defeated.

Bundled up one evening in a *Frozen*-themed comforter, I lay awake looking around the room. It was dark, but the moonlight seeping through the window allowed me to see the walls dressed with colorful pictures and the desk covered with coloring books and stickers. I remember feeling jealous of my niece's life. I thought *how wonderful it would be to have days filled with wants and desires*. In those few weeks of being home, my happiest moments were when she would steal me away from my computer to play board games with my family. She showed freedom in her choices and actions, as she was foreign to the idea of expectations. This silly concept helped me realize the pressure I'd put myself under. That night I asked myself, but *why?*

Why? This was a question I had yet to ask. For months I spent countless hours thinking about what my next step would be, when it would happen and where it would lead me.

I began to look at the expectations haunting me and asked *why* they had been set in the first place. I looked back at my failures and successes and the expectations set forth in those instances. I considered the *why* behind my mission to achieve each standard. As I flushed through this and began reflecting on my current situation, it dawned on me. I had allowed many of my adolescent insecurities morph into a defeating belief system, leaving me exhaustively striving to meet unhealthy expectations.

I realized the reason behind my urge to succeed was often to *prove* my worth, whether it be to myself or others. Those moments of feeling overwhelmed and disappointed were the result of unhealthy expectations, sabotaging my happiness. For too long I had been unable to savor small successes with fear of losing time from reaching the next one.

In that moment I decided I would no longer allow expectations, extending from insecurities, to haunt me. I knew the hopes for my life needed to be rooted in passions and desires. That night, in bed, I switched things up.

Like I do best, I began to make a list. I grabbed a pen and paper and wrote out my passions and my most genuine desires for what I loved and what I wanted to do in the world. These items would be my **why**. They would be the reason and purpose behind my hard work and the expectations I would aim to achieve. It wasn't until I did this that I was able to plan my next move.

Here's the thing about expectations…

Expectations help us establish a sort of playbook to live by. When you know your starting point and your end goal, expectations help you strategize your route.

However, when expectations don't stem from a positive place, as mine did not, the impact on your actions can be damaging. Whether it's a personal expectation or societal, when it's unhealthy, you risk losing sight of your actual goals. You may start working to fit a mold of what you believe you *should* be doing, rather than what you want to do. In these instances, you adapt to norms and risk falling further away from your true self. I've heard this type of behavior referred to as chameleon-like.

Confining yourself to the parameters of expectations creates risk of disappointment. Rather than allowing an expectation to dictate your mindset and every move, be flexible and willing to pivot. When you allow expectations to be restrictive and/or permanent you risk the ability to change goals when life doesn't go as planned, which we all know is expected.

My best advice to guide you through creating healthy expectations is, look back at the *why*. That playbook may show you everything else, but it is up to you to develop the purpose behind your actions and goals. Think about it, if you were to consider the *why* before conforming to an expectation, perhaps the risk of ingenuine actions could be avoided.

Looking back at purpose, which I like to call Operation Why, allowed me to solidify my passion. *Sharing purposeful stories to create positive impact.* Rather than using expectations to play on my insecurities, I now use them to honor myself and to fulfill my passions and dreams.

In the past year, I have had the pleasure of sharing over one hundred stories of people and communities, through my work with different publications across various mediums. This book, for example, allowed me to use my skills in journalism to aid women, in creating powerful narratives to share their personal stories and lessons learned.

Today, I'm earning my Master's Degree in Data Journalism at Stanford University. I am one of only 18 students in my program, working to develop skills in a pioneering field to produce content that promotes truth and understanding of complex societal issues.

Here are steps to help get you on the right track too:

Operation WHY:

1. Make a list of goals. Don't include any time limits. We don't need that pressure now.

2. Next to each goal, list the reason why you would like to meet this expectation.

3. Evaluate that column. Ask yourself are these words filled with things I love to do and interactions that bring me joy? Or are these expectations set by society, things I believe I "should" do, or rooted in an insecurity?

4. Next, cross out all of the expectations that involved things you believe you "should" do, unless of course they correlate with a true passion and are absolutely necessary. For those rooted in insecurities, is there a way to reframe these? Rather than doing something to prove I am the best at _____. Can you instead change the intention to meeting a goal because you are passionate about _____? Try it!

5. At the end of your operation you should have a list of fair, realistic and passion-filled expectations to work towards. Will every single action made from here on out be fun and exciting? Probably not. But, you will have deep-rooted purpose reminding you why you are working hard.

I must add that I struggled tremendously to write this chapter. As a journalist and writer, it is ironic to think that after years of capturing the stories of others I would find trouble sharing my own story. Please understand the tremendous value in each of our stories and how they've come to intertwine. As you take away a number of the lessons from this book, perhaps reframing your expectations, allow them to impact your interactions with others. Further, look at how they may influence the relationship you have with yourself. Now go on and continue to write the story of your life with passion and love. Go on, make it brilliant!

TWEETABLE

Look at the intention behind your goals, squash unhealthy expectations and free your soul to actions filled w/ genuine purpose #OperationWhy

Bethney Bonilla is a multimedia journalist and M.A. student in the Data Journalism Program at Stanford University. A passionate storyteller, she has crafted content promoting truth and understanding for outlets—including The Fresno Bee, KMPH FOX26, Peninsula Press and more. Beth acted as literary editor for the Passionistas book and is dedicated to sharing stories focused on social justice and human rights. Learn More: bethneybonilla.com

Tweet/IG: @bethney_bonilla

Contact: bethney.bonilla@gmail.com

Escaping From Literal and Metaphorical Jail

By Rachel S. Lee

Just how my friends would explain to me during our late night "kickbacks," the freezing cold holding cell had grey cement floors and rusty silver bars. There I was, alone in a cell, talking back to the cops, laughing in their faces. I knew the protocol was that I would be let out in a few hours because it was my first time in there. Too bad they took away my phone, or else I would have taken plenty of selfies. I was thinking to myself that I was SUCH a rebel—a rule breaker, a risk taker, a trouble maker. So Instagrammable!

I knew all of my friends were going to think I was such a gangster when I got out. I was right. I was now even cooler among my circle of friends. I felt invincible and was ready for more adventure and risk. I thought if I could handle that night, I could handle anything.

That was my mindset at 19 years old. The high of breaking the rules empowered me to believe that I could do whatever I wanted and achieve whatever my heart desired. Although I was still attending my college classes and my part time job, my priorities were: parties, drinks, hangovers, drugs, shoplifting, breaking the law—not to mention the free trips to jail. Things were either going to stay the same, get worse, or get better. They had to get better, right?

They got worse. A few months later, I found myself in jail again. Except this time it wasn't the city holding cell. I landed myself in county jail…"big girl" jail. I had to take out all of my piercings and shower in front of 20 strangers before they took me upstairs to meet my new roommates. We all matched in our orange shirts and pants. This was not one of those out of body, dream-like experiences. It felt real with each second slowly passing by. On my top bunk, a girl with tattoos on her face told me how she stole cars for a living. She offered me her boyfriend's phone number in case I wanted to get into that business when I got out. I no longer felt like a badass.

I felt out of place, but I wasn't scared. I was more fearful of what would happen when I got out and back into the real world where I would have the freedom to make choices. Bad choices came so easily. It was like I had an addiction to self-sabotage. Or a need to fit in with the crowd I affiliated myself with. If I didn't make changes in my choices, prison was next for me. Not bootcamp, not being grounded, not detention, but prison. It was at that moment I felt the full responsibility of my life and understood that I was not a child anymore, but an adult.

In order for me to change the direction of my life, I had to get clear on the life that I did want to live. I needed to visualize a compelling future to work toward. It wasn't until later that I discovered the power of journaling. At that time, I was lucky enough to use the internet to help me visualize. I started searching colleges that I wanted to go to and then found a beautiful one. I felt that I needed to move out of the town and environment I was in to help me commit to my new, healthy lifestyle. I also started doing online research about the town, apartments, restaurants, and community events. I wanted to get excited and have high anticipation for my move. I signed up for the community college and a few weeks later I got an acceptance letter to join the university for the following semester. I had a lot to look forward to.

I also created virtual, private vision boards on Pinterest and Instagram. I scoured lifestyle blogs and the social media profiles of women who were living a life similar to the one I wanted. I started to edit my own identity on social media and that also helped me step into being the person I wanted to be.

The process wasn't instant, but overtime, I have become a great decision-making machine, multi-passionate entrepreneur, Transformational Coach, Neuro Linguistic Programming (NLP) practitioner, author, and speaker. This happened through my ability to make thousands of seemingly small choices that were focused on my overall goals and vision for now and the future.

I use Neuro Linguistic Programming techniques and tools for myself and my clients all the time. I use NLP to discover the higher purpose of why my clients make certain choices and decisions in their lives. We look at why and how they are at the place they are at. We also dive deep into identifying a clear vision of person they need to be to take the actions they already know they need to be taking.

When reflecting on your life and choices (or those of someone you love) you must know what the meaning of a choice is and get down to the root of why those choices are being made. A choice is a decision that you commit to. Deciding and committing means no going back, burn the ships, there are no other options. We all have to make many decisions and choices every single day, and your ability to exercise your decision-making muscles will determine your successes.

Self-sabotaging decisions and habits are often our default and it takes the rewriting of our subconscious mind to make better conscious choices. In addition, the right choice is not always clear nor is it always easy to make.

This is true for all aspects of our lives including, but not limited to: health, work, relationships, habits, and finances. Where in your life is the devil on your one shoulder contradicting with the angel on your other shoulder? What is the higher purpose of the choices?

This scenario of devil and angel shows up in our lives every single day. Every single day you need to make choices. Do you make the empowering ones or disempowering, self-sabotaging ones? The empowering choices move you forward a few small steps and the disempowering ones set you back miles.

Self-sabotage often comes in the form of procrastination or pushing your dreams off until later. We dread doing the work such as going to the gym, making the phone call, or writing the article. But the truth is that just getting started is the hardest part. Once you begin, the weight of anxiety will be lifted off your shoulders.

Another form of self-sabotage is celebrating before we have anything to celebrate! This could be choosing to hang out with your friends or go on a date before you completed your responsibilities. This could be by overly drinking or spending money frivolously. You know the right choice is to work for your reward, yet so often we reward ourselves before accomplishing our goals.

I always tell my clients and my online audience that living a happy, successful life is hard work, but it's even harder work to live an unhappy, unproductive, self-destructive life. Putting your energy into the activities that will move you forward will keep you safe, happy, and an inspiration to others. It's never too late to grow up and take the actions you need to take to create the mindset shift you need. Whether that is reading self development books, going to empowering events, watching inspirational Youtube videos, or hiring a coach, the perfect time to start is now.

TWEETABLE

Make a 360 in your life at any moment with awareness and purpose
—Rachel S. Lee #transformyourreality #passionistas

Rachel S. Lee's mission is to help entrepreneurs be their authentic, unapologetic badass selves. In addition to her coaching and training business, Rachel owns an internet marketing firm, goboldmarketing.com Rachel teaches over 100 social media workshops per year. You will usually find her traveling to events, conferences, and seminars, to either learn, teach, or network. She is happily obsessed with the attainment of new knowledge and emotional fitness. You can find more at rachelslee.com.

How I Got My Groove Back

By Maria Mizzi

The idea of getting into the fitness field began when I was in college almost 20 years ago. I was working for a private gym in Beverly Hills. I worked at the desk so I was introduced to some amazing trainers to the stars. Seeing the results from the dedication of both the client and trainer was so exciting. Years later I would take that dedication into my own life when I found myself 30 pounds overweight, unhappy, and unhealthy. I would take this example with me as the formula for seeking results in all aspects of my life.

Although I loved fitness, a career in fitness was not yet in full focus. I began working in financial banking after college. During this time, we decided to also move to New York, where I continued my banking career. Working in the financial field meant long hours, a lot of sitting and, of course, there was always food to snack on in the break room. One day I realized I was stuck in a body I was not happy with. I was out of shape, feeling unhealthy and not fitting into my clothes. I didn't know how long it would take to get back my health and the body I wanted. I wasn't making the right choices with food or exercise and I was afraid to step on the scale.

I enjoyed working with banking clientele, but I still had the fire in me to do more with health and fitness. I knew I needed to get my personal health and body back first, so I spent much of my lunch hour learning more about fitness and food. Once I focused my energies on what I hoped to achieve, it was time to make a shift. I put together a program for myself, with those Beverly Hills folks in mind.

If those days at the receptionist desk taught me anything it was that the key to change was dedication and consistency. I decided to sign up for a 10K race in my hometown of Northport. I knew this would keep me on track both physically and mentally. I could not remember the last time I ran a mile. This is when I realized I also needed to be patient. Before I could run a 10K, I had to get my mind and heart in it too.

I developed the knowledge and ability to understand what needed to be done to get rid of those extra 30 lbs I gained. Ironically, just as I started training for this 10k, my husband's company took us to a Tony Robbins event. At the event, I learned why I felt as though I had no control over my weight and health. I had thought up a negative perception of myself over the years, slowly gaining weight, as many of us women do.

After attending, I immediately started to follow some of the advice to change that vision of myself. I started to write down what I wanted back and how I would take control of my weight and run this race. I started to feed my mind good thoughts and put together a step-by-step method. This was not easy at first. I began by creating a food journal, where I also wrote down how I felt before and after I would eat a meal. This is when I began to see what I was really hungry for. Food was masking my unhappiness in my hectic career and life I had created. I knew I had to make a change because my health and happiness continued to decline rapidly. I knew it was possible and I now had the tools to dedicate myself to getting healthy. It wasn't easy, but the other option meant I would continue down a dark road of disease and despair.

The dedication to my new program and race not only helped me gain confidence because I once again felt and looked good in my jeans, but it helped me seek results to my overall well-being. I ran over that finish line healthier, happier, more fit, and with the desire to help other women do the same.

In time, I decided to leave my banking career, go back to school, get certified in fitness and nutrition, and find a place to use my skill and passion. As soon as I made the leap, I knew, once again, results and success would come from dedication. I worked at the Personal Training Institute, where I learned from other amazingly dedicated trainers.

After a year of being in a gym setting, I wanted to craft more ideas for training clients towards seeking success. So I did! My husband is one of my huge success stories. He was a partner with a large firm, worked long hours, and ate terribly because of it. We worked together for a year making changes in daily food choices, implementing a consistent exercise routine, and a positive dedicated mindset that quickly progressed. One hundred and fifteen pounds later my husband was back to his high school weight! Years later, he is still at this weight, continuing with the Beach Physique Healthy Lifestyle and enjoying life, food, and fitness. Supporting him on his journey to health also helped me lose those last stubborn pounds, getting me into top fitness shape.

As a certified transformational nutrition and fitness coach, I have helped hundreds of women (myself included) gain back their confidence and live a happy, healthy lifestyle. I know what making small changes, hard work, and dedication has done for me and my clients, above and beyond losing weight.

I took the enlightenment I saw those days working in a private gym to inspire my journey towards success. Dedication was key. While it is not easy to maintain, here are some tools that keep me going:

- First, it's important to understand what is in your kitchen and what you are eating everyday. It's time to enjoy whole fresh foods, like vegetables, fruits, and lean meats.

- Second, is to begin moving daily. Staying consistent means walking daily then adding in strength training.

- The next important step is to sleep, real quality sleep.

- Finally, it is just as important to stop and simply enjoy time with yourself. Enjoy things like the outdoors and writing daily affirmations.

Dedication to these four steps helped me get my body, mind, and soul fit for life. Following these simple steps made those big changes I desired. Small changes make a big difference when you are dedicated to seeking results.

 ## TWEETABLE

Transformation is as simple as making small changes with consistency and dedication.
—Maria Mizzi #makeithappen #passionistas

 *Transformational Nutrition and Fitness Coach Maria Mizzi helps professional women make simple shifts in how they think about food and exercise to finally live that dream of a 10 plus life full of self-confidence, health and happiness both inside and out.*

www.MariaMizzi.com

https://www.facebook.com/BeachPhysiqueFitness/

https://www.instagram.com/beachphysique/

Bossbabe into ZENbabe

By Jeanette Ortega

There I was, inside my amazing, 5,000 square foot gym yearning to do more out in the world. I had accomplished what I had always wanted, to own my own gym, but I felt like something was missing. My niche was teaching a hard kick-ass boot camp. People would come to my facility knowing that they would get one of the best intense workouts. They would leave drenched with the sweat that they worked so hard for, exhausted yet pumped because they achieved something they thought was impossible. I love to see the body transform and people pushed to their limits while striving for a better them, but it all starts with the mind. Our mind-body connection is so strong and most people don't realize it. As people came in and out of my gym I started to notice a trend, the mind, body, soul connection was missing.

All through my years as a trainer, fitness competitor and business owner it was all about "hitting it hard" and "being the best." This mentality helped me win and become a WBFF Bikini Pro and celebrity trainer while building my LA gym Extreme Results Fitness, but at a price. I became unaware of my own mind, body, soul connection. I left it unattended until I came to a breaking point; my body and mind were breaking down at a rapid pace. Running a business, training to compete on a national and international fitness stage against the best of the best was tearing down my soul. There was no time for stillness or peace; it was always a constant PUSH for more.

At the point of my breakdown I was blessed. I trained an amazing client from Indonesia and she was so grateful for how I helped transform her life that she graced me with a two-week trip back to her country with her. This trip changed my life. It was there that I found my peace, my stillness, my ZEN and there that my heart and soul were reinvigorated.

I was taking a yoga class up in a tree that overlooked the beauty of Bali. I remember staring at what was before my eyes being so present in nature that all I could do is cry. It brought me back to my love of mind, body and soul. That is what my true meaning of fitness is. It's not how heavy you can lift, how many burpees you can do in a minute, or how many titles and trophies you win…it's about being balanced in mind, body and spirit. THIS is what I brought back to all my clients at my gym. I was at peace and I didn't care about success or the bottom line anymore. I was about going deeper into the heart and soul of my clients to transform them from the inside out.

We started health and wellness masterminds, meditation workshops, nutrition workshops, breathing workshops, fashion and recipe blogs and more! Just by doing this my business increased and people started dropping weight and becoming healthier in mind and body. We started 21-day challenges at the gym with the focus of "I AM." I am strong, I am motivated, I am dedicated, and I am courageous were just some of the statements being made. We created accountability teams, gym partners and more.

The entire energy of the gym shifted as I shifted, As I created more space for yoga, love and stillness, so did my clients. To me, being a Boss Babe is leading by example, creating and holding space for others and raising other leaders. As the gym focus shifted, my staff changed, more people with my same vision where being called in. My own focus became about being more "ZEN." I focused on allowing the flow of my life, and being consciously aware of all my decisions, my speech, and my thoughts. I went from a bad ass to a peace warrior and I've never looked back. This transformation happened at the perfect time and place and I am forever grateful.

As a result of this journey I am currently taking health and wellness of mind, body and soul global with my humanitarian efforts to Belize and around the world. Nothing is ever impossible! Own who you are and what you stand for. My Boss Babe tip: Never allow your business, your goals, your relationships, or anything rob you of your true inner peace. Allow time to create space for your mind, body and soul to be re-awakened on a daily basis.

TWEETABLE
Allow time to create space for your Mind, Body and Soul to be re-awakened on a daily basis.
—Jeanette Ortega #passionistas

Jeanette is a health & wellness expert, writer and fitness model, owner of her own gym "Extreme Results Fitness," creator of her own training method "Bootoga," celebrity trainer, and WBFF Bikini Pro. Contact her at extremefitchic@gmail.com

Passion The Wildfire

By Rebekah Wilson

Passion overtakes me the same way a wildfire runs rampant through a dry forest.

There is no stopping it.

There is no denying the flame.

Fire is warmth.

It is raw.

It is free willed.

A slight wind and the fire may change its course.

It is unstoppable in whatever path it may choose.

And even the fire does not know where its final destination may be.

Fire doesn't care about the finish line. It is about the journey.

Some see fire as destructive.

Others see the light that it brings to darkness.

They see the spark that can save lives with fire's warm flame.

But you can't have one without the other.

The same flame that holds the key to survival for many can also destroy lives if out of control. What does that mean for me?

The one who feels ablaze with a fire so bright; a passion that runs deep and strong.

TWEETABLE

Entrepreneurial Passion. There is no stopping it, there is no denying it, it is raw and free willed, running deep and strong.

Rebekah Wilson is an equestrian trainer and rider. She began riding professionally in the hunter/jumper world at age 20. She is passionate about fashion, sports, travel, fitness, the outdoors, and animals.

She is the founder of JDV, "joie de vivre," meaning the exuberant enjoyment of life, her personal consulting business where she assists those looking for a blueprint in the fashion, event, and travel industries.

Email: rjwilson.jdv@gmail.com

Facebook: RebekahWilson

Overcoming the Statistics

By Angeles Aguilar

I am who I am today because I had the passion to supersede statistics that challenged me.

Many of us face moments in our lives when data creates a daunting reality, numbers and probabilities that may or may not favor our aspirations and dreams. Since birth my life has been a constant fight against the odds.

After 16 hours of labor my mother finally gave birth to a weak baby girl with umbilical cord entanglement and noticeable signs of fetal distress. Even though the struggle for life had made way through my lungs, which for the first time were inhaling fresh air, the challenges ahead were not minor.

Forty days after I was born, I had to be hospitalized. This situation was like a bucket of cold water for my novice mother. I needed surgery. According to medical tests I had pyloric stenosis, a condition present in three out of 1,000 babies, which, without surgery, can lead to death. Food plainly and simply did not reach my stomach, so it was surprising I had survived so many days without nourishment. Fortunately, under the care of my mother and my grandmother, "Mama Yola," a miracle occurred. For the second time I survived in spite of the gloomy statistics.

I like to believe that at the time my tiny soul was fighting through those struggles knowingly. Whether that be the case or not, from those moments on, I gained strength in life. I overcame every rare disease and every onslaught that existence brought along. Before my infantile eyes a world full of possibilities was opened, where any obstacle could be overrun.

In spite of my passionate spirit and cheerful nature, my childhood was not so easy. As it happens to three out of ten children, I was prey of child bullying because of my parents' divorce. However, I discovered mysterious ways to brighten my days through music, reading, and a voracious imagination. Sitting in the classroom, I daydreamed about my adventures as a great gymnast, ballet dancer, and rock star, which immediately led my mother to buy a tutu and to enroll me in singing lessons. She has always been my principal mentor and taught me that everything we wish for can be achieved.

In a fantasy and dream environment, together with my mother's support, I started to write about all kinds of marvelous adventures, which turned more complex and more mature every time. My enjoyment for writing and journalism came to me at a very young age. Holding my father's hand, who was a reporter, I experienced for the first time the draft of a newspaper. I remember the hysteria, the implacable sound of the telephones, the smell of ink and the hypnotizing purring of hustle and bustle. How could I not fall in love with journalism?

And, in this world that was being revealed to me, in which letters, like paintbrushes, were portraying the reality and even, in the hands of experienced artists, challenging it, there was nothing to think over. I had found my element; the tutu, the soccer ball, and the tennis lessons in which my mom had very diligently enrolled me were left behind. As the one who falls in love for the first time, I grasped the objects of my affection, pencil and paper. What followed were happy years in which my pleasure in writing and research flourished. Time is the best teacher; it widened my wealth of knowledge, feelings, and emotions. My spirit was getting stronger while I was learning.

Later on, I enrolled in the university to get a communications degree with the goal of becoming a great journalist. However, my father, who worried about the exhausting life of reporters, instructed me to find another line of work. Alas, another statistic crossed my path. The beacon that had guided my steps so far was getting lost in the fog and rebellion was battering my soul. In the midst of the storm, my drifting boat took me to explore the world.

I visited Cuba, Spain, Turkey, and every corner of the world that my limited student budget allowed me. I took photography, art, and cinematography courses. I went to missions for a while, in order to disappear from the planet. Together with good friends and the music of The Doors, Pearl Jam, and The Smashing Pumpkins I was wandering around the world as an absolute rebel. I surrounded myself with plastic artists, filmmakers, dancers, and musicians and discovered that behind every door I knocked on there was a hidden story and every look taught me a lesson.

My attempt to get away from journalism only got me closer to my passion. I wrote all the time about the people I met on the road and about politically incorrect philosophic, social, and religious topics. My thoughts flowed and my free naked fingers in front of the keyboard seemed to be haunted. My passion for journalism came alive with every letter. What fascinated me even more so was the fact that journalism is not only words. It is the capacity to demystify a situation. It is a light against dark ignorance and the satisfaction that responds solely and exclusively to the truth.

My father, who in his time was also a rebel, saw in my eyes this enthusiasm for information, this flame that simply would not burn out. Finally, he agreed to stand beside his journalist daughter, a victory that over time led me to become a business reporter. However, beyond that victory, odds were still against me because statistics showed that just one third of journalists are women. Even in the US women face a glass ceiling, as there are only three female editors among the twenty-five largest daily newspapers. Meanwhile, the business world is still dominated by men.

Furthermore, my limited knowledge in economic topics rose as a great wall between my passion and me. Financial news is not lent to just any writing hand and it seemed mine was vetoed. I took statistics lessons, sought advice from my cousin the financialist and thoroughly browsed "Saint Wikipedia," but it all seemed a lost task. I took introductory courses and devoured books about economy, but I understood just half of some of them. Until one day, just like any other one, I took the reins of my destiny and decided to change. I hadn't let statistics dictate my life before this moment and I wouldn't do so now. I knew my passion and hard work was strong enough to push me through.

As someone jumping from "La Quebrada" in Acapulco, I plunged into a new educational adventure and decided to study a Master's Degree in Economics. What a struggle! I had never before been so dedicated. I listened to all my classes attentively, reviewed all afternoon, and approached my teachers for additional counselling. With time, my teachers, who at the beginning saw me like an outsider, accepted me into their community, as a respected student and friend. I graduated from Oxford Brookes Economics filled with glory.

Not only was I the pioneer in my family in studying a master's degree, I also joined the 4% of Mexicans with a postgraduate degree. If that was not enough, I studied away from home in another language and out of my comfort zone. I felt as though there was no bridge I could not build and no statistic I was not able to overcome.

I came back to Mexico and forged my way through the big door of business journalism. My new abilities gave me the opportunity to interview and meet chiefs of state, cabinet members, and CEOs of big multinational corporations. The stories of leaders, entrepreneurs, and big corporations caught my attention and nourished my spirit. I was enriched by so many people and decided to photograph this world that was inaccessible for so many.

My father, who used to be the biggest opponent to my vocation, became my greatest supporter and an outstanding mentor. He continues to motivate and challenge me everyday to improve. It is precisely that obsession for personal growth, the enthusiasm for information, and my professionalism that allowed me to climb the ladder of journalism and get hold of a solid reputation.

Chances are that, like me, you will probably find that at different stages of life statistics will battle your plans, your hopes, and your dreams. Recognizing those percentages is not easy. But, they cannot dictate who you are or your path. How you approach them will make all the difference and define on which side of the calculation you're going to be standing.

After a bumpy road and against the odds, I managed to become Angeles Aguilar, business journalist and story collector. This happened because, at the end of the day, passion for life understands very little about statistics.

TWEETABLE

At the end of the day, passion for life understands very little about statistics
—Angeles Aguilar #beattheodds #passionistas

Angeles Aguilar is the "go to girl" on financial topics in Mexico. In 10+ years in journalism, she has worked in print, TV, radio and new media. You can read her daily business column at La Razón, watch her economic insights on Proyecto 40, or watch her weekly spots for TV Azteca, one of Mexico's biggest TV networks. In her spare time, you can find her gardening in México City with her dog or holding hands with her husband Pepe.

aguilar.thomas.3@gmail.com

Twitter: @angelesaguilart

No Storm Lasts Forever

By Marissa Jones

"The beauty of a storm is that it comes in and clears out everything that is not rooted with a strong foundation," the words echoed in my head as the reality of it all became clear. Things and people I had devoted myself to were no longer serving me. The tighter I held on the more it all seemed to slip away. I sat there stunned at just how far from my truth things had become.

At 17 I traveled from one side of Texas to the far other side of the state to attend my dream school, Texas Tech University. It was time for dorm life, sorority life, learning, laughing, freedom, new friends, old friends, tailgating, football games, parties, fundraisers, and all-nighters. It was an amazing life, but it wasn't enough, I knew I wanted more.

Time flew by, a couple of years passed and somehow I found myself living in chaos. I was living in what felt like a mad house with four other girls, two dogs, a cat, the constant company of friends, neighbors, and latest boyfriends. That summer I was eager to move to my own one bedroom for a fresh start with my closest of friends around. No more painful reminders of lost friendships from an untimely fight. My new little home, all to myself, was exactly what I was looking for. That was, until the summer ended. I had just settled into my new place, when my circle of friends had to leave to return to school or to be with family. Next to make their exit was the man I had been dating, the one I devoted all of my time and energy to, who suddenly decided it was time for us to go our separate ways. Within just a few days everyone that had been a part of my daily life was gone all at once. The silence and emptiness of my new home became deafening. The following weeks I struggled to keep up with my classes and grades. My job at the local restaurant emotionally drained me day after day. I was feeling lost, with no purpose, and no connection.

Scrolling through Facebook passing the time, distracting myself, as I seemed to be doing more and more, I saw "No storm lasts forever. No struggle lasts forever. It's not here to stay." The words posted above the video woke up something inside me. I sat there and realized with such clarity what I had been ignoring; the truth in my heart, and the voice of my soul, and the pain I had been trying to numb. That video changed everything for me.

"What we resist, will persist," I let it sink in, as I understood it was time to surrender myself to that moment. Surrender myself to the breakdown. For months, I had been wanting to create something powerful and significant in my life. What I hadn't been able to see was that the universe had already been clearing me out for my true desires. Everything I was going through was preparing me for exactly what I had asked for. The experience of that moment was a wash of relief, I could finally walk away from what I had been trying to hold on to and control.

The next morning, I found myself with a newly discovered energy and motivation to create and make the most of this vision and opportunity. I knew it was time to leave. It was time to flip my world upside down if I was really going to do this right. I searched the maps looking for the destination of my new beginning.

A year later, I'm living on the other side of the world in Sydney, Australia, preparing to go to France with the wonderful man I've fallen in love with and whom I am so grateful to share these experiences with. I'm continuing to finish my degree from Texas Tech University through online classes. I'm working on my TEFL certificate so that I can continue to travel and pursue my passion of volunteering and working with kids. And the man who created that video, the video that changed it all for me, I'm grateful to call him my personal coach and mentor now. Over this last year I have seen parts of the world I could never dream of, I have met the most unexpected people, I have lived in the most surprising places, I have learned countless things about myself, I have chosen to live my life out of love with a sense of purpose instead of choosing to live in fear.

The beauty of a breakdown is that there is no pain without purpose, whether it is a lesson learned or a prayer answered. Embrace these moments because it's not about trying to get it right, it's realizing that you could never get it wrong. In the end, it's about trusting your intuition, taking those leaps of faith, losing and finding happiness, and embracing life as it unfolds before you.

"Ever since my house burned down, I see the moon more clearly."

—Gregory Colbert

TWEETABLE

Embrace these moments because it's not about trying to get it right it's realizing you could never go wrong.
—Marissa Jones #passionistas

Marissa Jones is a writer and Teaching English as a Foreign Language (TEFL) teacher majoring in communications at Texas Tech University. She is a long-time volunteer at the Women's Protective Services Shelter of Lubbock, TX where she enjoyed working with children and organized several fundraisers. You can find Marissa sipping coffee under the Eiffel Tower, sailing beyond the Great Barrier Reef, and tasting paella in Seville.

Contact at marissajones.m@gmail.com.

Technology and Your Potential

By Talia Fuhrman

We live in a time in which we can share as little or as much of our lives as we want to with the world. Not only do we get to choose the type of person we show up as in everyday life, but we also get to choose how much of ourselves to broadcast and the image we wish to portray on social media regardless of how happy we are on the inside. The technology age and all of the accessories that come with it (social media, smartphones, a world of information and articles online) come with pros and cons depending on how we use them. With such a flood of information, life can get confusing. There are so many choices, so many ways to spend your time. What do you value?

It has never been more important to have the right role models and close friends in the real world. As you read the following paragraphs, keep in mind that my obstacles have been many, but none have stopped me and I can thank my close relationships for keeping me inspired and motivated through every up and down.

I grew up in the world of athletics and as a teenager my goal was to become a pro tennis player. I was an ambitious little one and both my ambition and work ethic has stayed with me ever since. As I was very physically active from childhood onwards, what I fueled my body with was certainly on my mind. Not to mention, my father is one of the most recognized nutrition experts in the country.

One challenge has been finding my own way in an environment in which it would have been easy to follow directly in my father's footsteps. I cannot say that I've ever had one "aha" moment, but I've had many little ones that have grown and morphed in time. In my opinion, these little "aha" moments are just as vital, if not more so, than any big one.

What inspires us changes as we change. I've tried everything from acting to screen writing to fashion merchandising to environmental science. In college I finally switched my major back to nutrition after dropping film studies. You know you've found your passion when you put a lot of work into it simply because you love the challenge of the work. I always returned to nutrition because studying human health has been the most rewarding pursuit to date.

I have one book under my belt called *Love Your Body*, which was published by Rodale Publishing Inc. in September 2014. That book began because of my own experience overcoming body image anxieties as a teen and early 20-something in addition to my perpetual captivation with nutrition. I began writing about the science of nutrition in my own enthusiastic tone in my spare time during my junior year of college and within those first few months of writing I decided I wanted to embark on writing a book. Recipes were added because I love experimenting in the kitchen and a chapter on the connection between factory farming and climate change is in there too. I went to a climate change conference in London in 2010 and there I found my fascination with the topic of factory farming and climate change burgeoning. I wanted to do something to help. I've always been an investigator with a curious mind at heart.

The entire time I was writing that book, I never knew if I was going to get a book deal. I didn't sign with a publishing company until the entire book was written and I was very lucky to be offered a deal given it was my first and I was just out of college.

Today I am finishing my second book, which is night and day from the first. The second book is a health desserts cookbook fused with poetry written on the topic of positive psychology. Since the first book was released, I've pursued more creative endeavors and fallen more in love with food photography and recipe creation. How did the second book unfold? I listened to my heart and didn't give up. I am still learning and growing in everything I do, be it in the world of writing, the culinary arts or photography. If I write anything about myself, it comes back around to the main point: each one of us should have the courage and fearlessness to go after a life we love regardless of any challenges we may face.

You may be wondering why I began writing about technology and then seemed to have neglected that topic as I began writing about my journey. Here I come back to it. Firstly, I have never shared on social media that the entire time my journey has unfolded I've lived in chronic pain. I hurt a nerve playing tennis when I was 17 years old and have been in pain ever since. I've been looking for a solution since that time and seem to be getting closer to figuring out what the solution is. Without getting into specifics, I haven't let that challenge stop me from anything I set out to do. I only share it with you here because one of the most important lessons we will ever learn is that we can overcome anything we set our mind to. Everything in life is perspective.

Secondly, I think how we use technology now will determine our own individual potentials. Don't let the clutter of what's out there distract you from your own path just as you cannot let the voices of others distract you from the voices that come from your heart. We all have our own journeys and this is what makes each one of us beautiful. Respect your own and never compare yourself to anyone else but you.

 TWEETABLE
We all have our own journeys and this is what makes each one of us beautiful. Respect your own and never compare yourself to anyone but you.

 *Talia Fuhrman is a twice published nutrition author, popular food blogger, and fashionista. She believes the true meaning of health and wellness comes not only from delicious, nutrient-rich foods, but also from the power of positive energy and zest for a truly fulfilling life. You can find Talia writing, reading and being creative in Southern California.*

Learn more: taliafuhrman.com

Instagram: taliafuhrman

Know Yourself, Love Yourself

By Tamiel Kenney

Life does not always go the way we hoped or planned. Sometimes it is not the fairytale ending we all dreamed about when we were little girls. The fact is, our life and how it turns out depends on us. We cannot change others around us. We can only make the necessary changes to ourselves, which is the starting point of creating that future you hope to obtain.

I was 20 years old in 1995 when I decided to marry my husband, Mark. I was young, but I thought I was old enough to make that choice. After all… wasn't that what every girl dreamed of? To get married, have a family and live happily ever after?

Problem was, I did not understand back then what I know very well now. You have to know yourself and be happy with who you are before you can join someone else's life and be happy with them. No one can MAKE YOU HAPPY…they can only add to or take away from your happiness if you allow them to. You must first love yourself or it will be extremely hard for anyone else to do so long-term.

This was a truth that I have come to know well. In 2012, after seventeen years of marriage, I was really struggling. Our marriage was struggling. We were under so much stress with Mark's IT business and stress from having to deal with GIRL drama (we had a couple girls live with us to help them start a new life after giving their babies up for adoption). This is another story in itself. How could I give these girls what they truly needed, when I had nothing to give? How could I help them see their value and purpose, when I did not see my own?

At this point I had considered separating from my husband. I did not feel that I was able to discover my own purpose in life when I was with him. At this point, we had two young children. Every time I started to make detailed plans in my mind about what a separation would look like and where I would live to create my "new life," I would have an uncontrollable emotional breakdown. I thought that there was something wrong with me.

The day that I had a breakdown in front of my children was the day I knew something had to change. I did not want to be the person I had become. I did not want the life I was starting to plan, apart from my husband, for myself or for my children. This was the day I decided to risk having a conversation with my husband that I didn't know how to have. We were in trouble and I was going downhill fast and something had to change NOW.

We decided to see a marriage counselor. She was wonderful—for the both of us. She taught us how to communicate with each other, something that neither one of us learned growing up. We learned that one of the biggest parts of being a good communicator is to be a good listener. Listen to the other person's perspective. Listen to their heart and how they feel...even if you don't understand the way they feel.

Sometimes things happen to us that change the course of our lives. Other times, we have to take action to change that course. Either way, the sooner you see the need for a course correction, the better. The sooner you know what actions you need to take to put you on that course, the better. If you know that something needs to change but don't know what to do to change it, find a mentor or someone who can guide you. Not just any mentor will do. Find someone who has had similar experiences or someone who shares your vision for the future that you want to create!

Let's move forward to 2013. Mark has had his own IT business for years and did really well in that world, a world I knew nothing about nor understood. He works very hard in everything he does, but I could not help him in this business. In 2013, we decided to start investing in larger multifamily apartments as a way to create passive income for our family. If anything were to happen to Mark, the cashflow of his business would be gone and the kids and I would have to fend for ourselves. So, we joined a group to meet other like-minded people. We met some great people in that group and have grown our portfolio to owning 1,300 units in three short years.

After three years of being in that group, we saw some dynamics we did not like. With most any situation there are things you like and things that you don't. Mark and I decided that the group did not provide an environment that would let our business thrive and did not allow us to control our own destiny. So, we made the decision to leave that group and venture out on our own.

Very shortly after leaving our educational group, many people started calling and emailing us. They would share their stories about how they were dissatisfied with their current business situations or dissatisfied with a mentor or guru they had paid thousands of dollars to and who did not provide all that they had promised. Mark and I very quickly felt a PASSION to help these people achieve the freedom that they were seeking.

People who know me, can confirm that I have always had a big heart to help others. Sometimes I would overcommit myself because I saw an unmet need. I have heard it said, "If not you, then who?" If I did not meet that need, who would? So, I attempted to help anyone I could.

After three years of investing in multifamily apartments ourselves and acquiring 1,300 units, Think Multifamily was born. Mark and I have always loved real estate and have found a way to share our passion together and to teach others about investing in real estate to build wealth and creating a legacy for themselves and their family.

We have grown so much since 2012, as individuals and in our marriage. Our kids see a big difference in us and our daughter, who is now 9 years old, is constantly teasing us for kissing or touching each other or just hugging each other in the short elevator ride down to the 1st floor in our apartment complex. We have learned to work together as a team, understanding that we both have strengths and weaknesses and that we can use each of our strengths to benefit ourselves and others.

Looking at where I am today, I am more confident now than I have ever been. I have learned to communicate well with others, although I can still improve in this area. I have learned to be a real PARTNER with my husband, in business and in life. We have learned to use our strengths collectively to build a better life together and help others improve their lives as well.

After almost twenty-two years of marriage (wow, that is a long time), we still have hiccups in our relationship, but we address them right away instead of letting things fester. We try to remember the communication skills that our counselor taught us and remember that our marriage relationship is number one (after our relationship with God), then the children, then our business and helping others. We are a team. We can help others out of abundance and cannot help others when we are empty. We have hired a new mentor who will help guide us in this next chapter of our lives and are connecting with others that have the same integrity and character that we value. We must first fill our tanks, find our passion and then take action to help others.

What is it that you hope to achieve in your lifetime? Don't let fear of the unknown hold you back from the great things the future holds for you. What is fear anyway but False Evidence Appearing Real. Once we realize our fears, only then can we take the steps necessary to overcome them. Then the whole world is ours! A new adventure awaits us around every corner! There is no time like the present to begin a new chapter in your life. Find your passion! Take action!

TWEETABLE:
What is it that you hope to achieve in your lifetime?
—Tamiel Kenney #FindyourPASSION #TakeACTION
#Servantleadership #passionistas

Tami and her husband Mark, co-founded Think Multifamily—a program to teach others how to invest in multifamily real estate with confidence. Having invested in over 1,300 apartments, they help others obtain the kind of success that they have achieved through living with integrity, authenticity and humility, as well as having a servant leadership focus.

To learn more about Think Multifamily, visit their website at www.thinkmultifamily.com

Email: Tami@thinkmultifamily.com

Facebook: Tamiel Kenney

From the Jungle to Big American Dreams

By Leslie Vera

Somewhere between wanting to make my parents proud, and having million dollar dreams I found the path I always envisioned for myself. I remember being 6 years old, leaving home to go to a parade by myself. I eventually joined in and became a part of it because that's what I really wanted to do. At 6 years old, I believed in doing the impossible to make your dreams come true. Since an early age I remember claiming my independence. I believed in the bigger picture and had the determination to achieve anything I put my mind to.

I come from a small town in the jungles of Peru. My family and I moved to the states when I was 9 years old; I still remember that day as if it was yesterday even though it's been 13 years now. From the moment I arrived in this country, my family focused on giving me the best education they possibly could. I attended a charter school from 7 a.m. to 5 p.m. from 5th grade until I graduated high school, and I was at the top of my class throughout all those years. My parents had a limiting criteria for what would make them proud, which was: me going to college, getting a stable job, and being financially "secure." The road was paved for me, and I knew exactly where I was going: college. However, everything changed when I started modeling at age 17.

I was introduced to a world and a lifestyle no one had ever shown me before. I was traveling for work, eating at the most expensive restaurants, and networking with successful people. I learned then the importance of putting myself in the right environments; environments that will help me grow. I was experiencing things some people only dream of experiencing in a lifetime. I knew this was the lifestyle I wanted for the rest of my life, but I also knew I wanted to make my parents proud. Although the box that my parents had put me in didn't align with how big my dreams actually were, I attended college as a bioengineer major and I kept modeling as a part time job. In the years to come, I learned valuable lessons from my short modeling career that have helped me keep moving forward in the entrepreneurial path I've chosen.

Having the opportunity to be around so many successful people taught me the importance of networking and building relationships. I took every opportunity to be around success. I was intrigued and curious to find out how the successful people I knew were made. In one conversation with one of my mentors, he said to me, "I could be having this conversation with anybody else, and they would not ask me the questions you are asking." That small comment engraved itself in my head and taught me the power of asking the right questions to the right people.

At the time, that meant not only finding out their system but also the "why" behind every move they had made that led them to have the lifestyle I wanted for myself. Jim Rohn once said, "You are the average of the five people you spend the most time with." This quote triggered the change of my circle of influence. I went from hanging out with my college friends to building relationships with people who were much more experienced than me and learning from them.

One of the other major keys to success I learned in the process is to always show up. Take every opportunity that the universe throws at you. It only takes one person to believe in you to change your life. Every event I've attended, and every opportunity I've taken, has always helped me move one step closer to my dreams of financial independence because of the people I was able to network with. Showing up is 80% of the work, and the other 20% is adding value which means showing up with a great attitude and giving as much as you can. Many times, the opportunity to put myself in those environments were not free. I had to learn to invest in myself if I wanted to be in the same room as the people who would then invest their time in me to teach me, and guide me through this journey.

My entrepreneurial spirit didn't begin when I met successful people though. When I was 10 years old, I started making bracelets that I would sell to my neighbors and friends for a dollar each. I knocked on doors showing my different designs, and I learned to take rejection very well. It taught me that if one person says no, I was just one knock closer from a person saying yes. This lesson would serve me well 12 years later. At age 22, I launched a startup in the technology industry. It took a few "nos" from investors to finally find someone who believed in me, my dreams, and passion. I designed and created an app that will revolutionize social media.

This app, FunItUp, helps you find people who want to do the same activities as you at the exact same time. We started the project earlier this year, and have networked our way to a database of over 7 million people to reach once the app is in the App Store. It has been the hardest I've ever worked and the challenges conquered have definitely taught me lessons one could only learn from experience. Needless to say, I don't have a regular 9-5 job, but my work hours are from the time I open my eyes in the morning until I lay in bed at night to go to sleep. Although I didn't get a job to be financially "secure," I learned that the people who really care and believe in you will be just as proud for following your dreams. If there's anything I want convey through my story, it is to always show up wherever your dreams take you. You never know who you're going to meet or the opportunities that will present themselves. If you show up with a great attitude and give as much as you can, God will take care of the rest. Believe in your vision, and don't let anyone discourage you from working on your dreams.

TWEETABLE
Always SHOW UP wherever your dreams take you!
—Leslie Vera #BelieveInYourVision #Passionista

Leslie Vera is a entrepreneur, real estate investor, and model. Her newest app FunItUp provides new ways to connect through the activities you love. She and her family moved from the jungles of Peru to the California when she was nine years old. Since then, she has worked hard towards making her dreams a reality. Visit FunItUpApp.com to learn more.

Happiness Is Closer Than You Think

By Marlene Wilkerson

Would you like ketchup or spicy mayonnaise for your french fries? Every time I asked this question I would then question myself. Do you really enjoy asking guests which condiments they prefer? As a college student, becoming a server at a trendy upscale Los Angeles restaurant was perfect. You work short shifts, interact with new people every day, and one night of tips were more than most college students' one-week paycheck. There came a time where running back to the kitchen to give that one picky regular, who likes two ice cubes (not one, or three, but two) in her drink and watching bickering couples who throw an iPad in their two-year-old's face to consume and distract him during dinner was just not worth the "good money." I had no purpose.

I was completely happy with being a server for my four years as a college student. Work was fun, "regulars" would request to sit with me, and I loved my job. In my last semester of my senior year in college I dreaded my shift, I was no longer happy walking into work, and I was highly irritable after. I hated always having to tie up my big curly hair is the smallest bun, wearing baggy slacks and keeping my nails the same "natural" color. When I put on my uniform I felt like I was taking "off" my personality; I had to tone "me" down. I was never this girl. I talked my coworkers and friends about my work situation, longing for help with my new uninterested attitude, but most of them just agreed telling me, "hating your job is normal." I found that very ironic because I would regularly serve four young women (around my age) who always talked about how they loved their jobs. They would come in a few times a week for lunch with new stories, business opportunities, and their Porsche and Mercedes Benz keys on the table. While I filled their water glasses, I would hear their conversations about stressing over which dress to wear for their business trip to Greece. So stressful right? I would then go to the back where most of the servers would hang out during down time and hear conversations about not getting their shift covered, stressing over picking up more shifts to pay for rent, and being completely drained from working double shifts but having finals the following week.

This was my turning point; I knew there was a clear and obvious choice to be made. I was going to be like those girls at the table. I did not want their Porsche or Mercedes Benz keys. I did not want to be them. I wanted happiness, fulfillment, and purpose. I wanted what their careers symbolized.

Freedom, vibrancy, and abundance. They had the success that most people believed was only obtainable for older experienced people. At this time, my mindset was fixed on that type of success only being available at an older age just because that is what most people around me thought. My first step was to eliminate limitations.

My attitude completely changed and I was happy again. I would come to work like my old self. I tied my hair in the smallest bun, wore baggy slacks, and had the same natural nail color. To everyone else I was a server, but in my head, I was my own boss. I worked for myself, came to work with the biggest curliest hair, stylish outfit, and bold accessories. Though I was delivering entrees, I was envisioning my business goals, planning out social media strategies, and picking out furniture for my penthouse apartment. As I would take orders I found myself daydreaming about my life of prosperity and ability to take spontaneous vacations. I often took "bathroom breaks" where I would write down every little hunch during my shift. Sometimes the hunches would have my fingers speed typing for five minutes losing track of the time. The reality was I did not have tangible possession of any of those things, I did not even have a business idea—yet.

I made major changes inspired by the teachings in the book "The Secret," and "Think and Grow Rich." I listened to audiobooks in the car, read every day, made a vision board, programmed my mind to think positively, and made a plan. At this point I still didn't have an exact business in mind. I didn't know what, how, or where I was going to get the idea but I knew that I would. The thought of convincing myself to go down a path and not knowing what was ahead made me insane. There were times where I would fall off of my plan and resort into thinking I was not capable of creating my own way. After a few failed attempts I held myself accountable and choose to persist to complete my plan.

When I made the commitment to stick to my plan my business idea casually slipped into mind. It was almost too easy. It seemed too good to be true. It came to me when I wasn't thinking about finding an idea; I wasn't working hard or even completing tasks for my plan. It just came to me. On the other side of completion was my answer. Through taking the time to trust myself and stay true to a plan, I found purpose. My mind knew exactly what I wanted and lead me to a way of making it all possible. Now, I truly believe in myself and any small, large, crazy, or absurd idea that comes to mind. I learned I have the power to create anything I want.

It is not hard to accomplish your goals, the hard part is making the decision to finally go for it. Once you do that that, it is yours. I simply just made the choice to be different than my surroundings. I separated myself from people and energy that were content with unhappy or less fulfilling lifestyles. Why would I work forty hours a week with no inner purpose when I could be working forty hours a week putting energy and focus to better my mind and goals. I get it, not everyone wants to be their own boss and have their own business, but everyone should be happy. Please remember happiness is closer than you think. Ask yourself what you want and your newfound happiness will be right on the other side. If you are unhappy with your job or career, that can easily change. I get to be me every day. I don't have to hide my hair, tone down my outfits, and be told what to wear. I am paid to become a better version of myself and to inspire others to do the same. Find your purpose. I choose to make my passion my paycheck. You can do the same.

TWEETABLE

It is not hard to accomplish your goals, it's hard to decide to finally go for it. There is no greater gift than living your calling.

Marlene Wilkerson is Founder of the The Find Guru an online boutique and fashion resource for fashion, hair, and fitness finds. She is a southern California native with a degree in Business Marketing who has always dreamed big with a positive, happy, compassionate mindset. Today, Marlene is a major social media influencer through The Find Guru with 166k followers on Youtube and 261k on Instagram. Learn more at thefindguru.com.

Youtube: The Find Guru

Instagram: @thefindguru and @goldennn_x

KIM SOMERS EGELSEE'S
10 WEEKS TO CONFIDENCE
HOW TO EXUDE CONFIDENCE IN EVERY INTERACTION

Receive a 2 Week All Access Trial to 10 Weeks to Confidence For Only $11.96

Go to 10WeekstoConfidenceTrial.com

▶ **Week One** – Living A Congruently Confident Life

▶ **Week Two** – Creating Confident Communication, States, Beliefs and Behaviors

▶ **Week Three** – Confidence Is Being in Alignment With What You Love

▶ **Week Four** – Move Forward With Bold Fearlessness

▶ **Week Five** – Making Space For Greatness

▶ **Week Six** – Connect And Collaborate For Confidence

▶ **Week Seven** – Embrace Your Uniqueness

▶ **Week Eight** – Believe And Achieve Your Power Goals

▶ **Week Nine** – Ask For What You Want

▶ **Week Ten** – Bring Your Confidence To The Table And Own It Every Time

Plus Receive 20 Powerful World-Class Confidence and Success Interviews!

10WeekstoConfidenceTrial.com

KYLE WILSON

Entrepreneur · Marketer · Strategist

"Kyle, thank you for our partnership and friendship. Friendship is wealth and you make me a rich man. You are the best!" **JIM ROHN**

- Founder Jim Rohn International
- Produced 100+ best-selling products
- Collaborated with industry legends
- Founder YourSuccessStore.com
- Founder LessonsFromNetwork.com

Download **FREE** Kyle's 52 Lessons I Learned From Jim Rohn and Other Legends I Promoted.

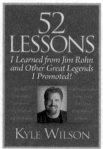

Receive FREE Kyle Wilson's

52 LESSONS I Learned From Jim Rohn and Other Legends I Promoted

To Access FREE go to KyleWilson.com/connect

Kyle shares Lessons he has learned from collaborations with Legend Jim Rohn as well as Brian Tracy, Darren Hardy, Jeffrey Gitomer, Les Brown, Og Mandino, Denis Waitley and more!

Plus Also Receive These Additional Bonuses

Promoter Kyle Wilson shares his Cliff Notes from the **Brian Tracy 3-Day Weekend** he put on. Includes Key Ideas from Brian Tracy, Darren Hardy, Erika De La Cruz, Ron White and more.

Receive FREE **Two-Time US Memory Champion Ron White's** eBook *How to Memorize Everything.* *Topics include how to memorize names, faces, speeches and more. $19.97 value*

Kyle Wilson interviews 20 year close friend and former **publisher** of *Success* Magazine Darren Hardy. Topics include Mentors, Marketing, Building Your Brand, Personal Development.

"I guard my endorsements carefully. Kyle, he is simply a marketing genius! He was the wizard behind Jim Rohn and other greats. Every marketing dilemma I have ever had Kyle has given me the brilliant and elegant solution on the spot. Kyle's consulting has saved and earned me hundreds of thousands of dollars over the years." —**Darren Hardy**

Access FREE – Go to KyleWilson.com/connect

KYLE WILSON'S
LESSONS FROM NETWORK

PROFESSIONALS · WOMEN IN BUSINESS · SELLING · INVESTING · SPEAKING · YOGA · MUSIC · AUTHORS · MARKETING · SPORTS · COACHES · SOCIAL MEDIA · HEALTH & FITNESS

A Community Connecting Life and Business Experts with the Marketplace!

Here is a Sampling of the Powerful Programs You Can Access on Topics including Marketing, Selling, Branding, Speaking, Leadership, Communication and more!

Brian Tracy
Success Mastery Academy

Darren Hardy
Productivity Secrets of Super Achievers

Erika De La Cruz
Assume Your Throne

Delatorro McNeal
Crush the Stage Explode Your Income

Seth Mosley
Parents Basement to Winning a Grammy

Nick Bradley
Habits of a Champion

Roy Smoothe
You Are Your Brand

Vic Johnson
Become the Celebrity Authority

**Kim Somers Egelsee's
Confidence Building
Course**
(4-part series)

**Heather Christie's
Executive Leadership
Coaching Model**
(4-part series)

**Eric Lofholm's
Sales & Prospecting
Persuasion & Influence**
(17-Part Series)

**Chris Widener's
Leadership Series**
(7-part series)

**Vic Johnson's
4 Basics of Building a
Online Business**
(4-Part Series)

**Bob Donnell's
Mastering Your Inner
Game**
(7-part series)

**Tony Teegarden's
Client Conversion Clinic**
(4-Part Series)

**Ron White's
Memory in a Month**
(34-Part Series)

Plus Access the LFN Resource Center, Expert Calls and Live Q&A Calls!

Plus Bonus Section including Ron White's Speed Reading, Robert Helm's Unlock True You Goal Setting, Kyle Wilson & Larry Thompson's Tribute to Jim Rohn and more.

Receive a 2 Week All Access Trial to the Lessons From Network For Only $11.96
Go to LessonsFromNetworkTrial.com

ABOUT THE AUTHOR

The Huffington Post begged the question in the article *How Telling Your Story Can Change Your Life* featuring Erika, *"Who* is this girl and why is she so happy?"

> *"Erika De La Cruz is a Media Personality, Speaker, Coach, Author, and Entrepreneur. That's a lot of commas, but, in my opinion, her most valuable title is that of an insanely positive person who wants nothing more than to help those around her."*

—Gregg Clunis: Huffington Post Contributor & Entrepreneur

Erika replied in a statement with the origin of who she really is.

> *"Let's see, who am I and why am I so happy? That's a way more fun question than "tell us what you've accomplished!" Well—yes. Most of the time, I'm happy, extreemlyyy happy. And bouncing around, using phrases like "juju" and "I love everyone." I call myself a "mainstream hippy." It stems from my belief that you can be spiritual and compassionate while also wearing designer labels and loving Taylor Swift. ☺ I have a very practical take when it comes to thought process and business, but at my core, I firmly believe that MAGIC exists and that you can manifest your dream life if you want to! Let's see, I'm a hugger versus a high-fiver, a girl who skipped hipster for couture, despite the growing trend. A girl who has a message of pure love and dream pursuit. Who wants to help move and inspire people toward greatness, who gets to be her "best self" for a living. A girl who loves media and film and aims to revolutionize the entertainment industry. A girl who is invested in shifting millennial mind-set for the better, through sharing her own story and experiences. And at the heart of it, well, I guess I'm a girl who listens to Disney Children's Pandora station whenever she can, who loves "yummy mugs," and wearing "matchies" in the winter (a term I coined for the coziest pajamas on earth). And finally, I'm a girl who believes: love, gratitude and action are the answers."*

—Erika De La Cruz: Co-Founder of *Passionistas, Tips Tales & Tweetables From Women Pursuing Their Dreams*

Are You A Passionista?

Hi there! Hope you enjoyed reading this book.

If you're convinced that your dreams are meant to be pursued, that your story should be shared, not kept a secret and that YES—you should be able to turn your inspiration to revenue like a boss, too.

DOING WHAT YOU LOVE...

then, it's time for you to become a passionista. I've curated an amazing community of fellow lady-bosses just like you! As well as a Boss-Babe Blueprint that will take you from cultivating your dream life to LIVING IT.

I'd like to invite you to learn more about our community and events by signing up for a *Passionista Strategy Session* where we will cover any or all of the following topics:

Vision, Your Story, Mind-Set, Press & Media, Business Blueprint and Spotlight Method Strategy.

Just follow this exclusive prospective passionista link:

http://www.passionistasbook.com
Book Your Free Strategy Session!